D0203700

REDEFINING LINGUISTICS

REDEFINING LINGUISTICS

Edited by

Hayley G. Davis
and Talbot J. Taylor

London and New York

Stafford Library
Columbia College
10th and Rodgers
Columbia, MO 65216

√410.1
R246

To Bill and Rosie

First published 1990
by Routledge
11 New Fetter Lane, London EC4P 4EE

Simultaneously published in the USA and Canada
by Routledge
a division of Routledge, Chapman and Hall, Inc.
29 West 35th Street, New York, NY 10001

Selection and editorial matter © 1990 Davis and Taylor
Individual chapters © 1990 the respective authors

Typeset by Columns of Reading
Printed in England by TJ Press (Padstow) Ltd,
Padstow, Cornwall

All rights reserved. No part of this book may be reprinted or
reproduced or utilized in any form or by any electronic,
mechanical, or other means, now known or hereafter invented,
including photocopying and recording, or in any information
storage or retrieval system, without permission in writing from
the publishers.

British Library Cataloguing in Publication Data
Redefining linguistics.
1. Linguistics
I. Davis, Hayley G.   II. Taylor, Talbot J.
410

Library of Congress Cataloging in Publication Data
Redefining linguistics / edited by Hayley G. Davis and
Talbot J. Taylor.
p.   cm.
Includes bibliographical references.
ISBN 0–415–05495–8. — ISBN 0–415–05496–6 (pbk.)
1. Linguistics—Methodology.   I. Davis, Hayley.   II. Taylor,
Talbot J.
P126.R4   1990
410′.1—dc20   90–8365
CIP

ISBN 0–415–05495–8
ISBN 0–415–05496–6 pbk

CONTENTS

CONTRIBUTORS

Hayley G. Davis is engaged in research at St Edmund Hall, Oxford. She has been a Visiting Lecturer in Linguistics at Roehampton Institute of Higher Education, and Assistant Professor in Linguistics at Northeast Missouri State University, where she was organizer of the conference 'Linguistics Redefined' in March 1989.

Roy Harris holds the Chair of English at the University of Hong Kong and is Emeritus Professor in General Linguistics at the University of Oxford. He is the author of the trilogy *The Language Makers* (1980), *The Language Myth* (1981), and *The Language Machine* (1987) published by Duckworth, and of *Language, Saussure and Wittgenstein* (Routledge: 1988).

Paul Hopper is Professor in Linguistics in the English Department at Carnegie Mellon University, Pittsburgh. He is the author of *The Syntax of the Simple Sentence in Proto-Germanic* (Mouton: 1975), and the editor of *Tense-aspect: between semantics and pragmatics* (John Benjamins: 1982), and *Studies in Transitivity* (with S. A. Thompson, Academic Press: 1982).

Nigel Love is Senior Lecturer in Linguistics at the University of Cape Town, South Africa. He is the author of *Generative Phonology: a case study from French* (John Benjamins: 1981), and the editor of *Foundations of Linguistic Theory: selected writings of Roy Harris* (Routledge: 1990).

Talbot J. Taylor is an Associate Professor in Linguistics in the English Department at the College of William and Mary, Virginia. He is the author of *Landmarks in Linguistic Thought* (with Roy Harris, Routledge: 1989), *Analysing Conversation* (with Deborah Cameron, Pergamon Press: 1987), and is the editor of *Ideologies of Language* (with John Joseph, Routledge: 1990).

1

INTRODUCTION

Hayley G. Davis

The academic discipline of linguistics is at a critical stage of development. Whatever consensus there may have been fifteen or even ten years ago is fast disappearing. A process of redefinition is already in the works (see Harris 1980, 1981, 1987b). The aim of this volume is to contribute to that process, and, in so doing, to explain why a redefinition is needed and, in some cases, how it should proceed. The contributors feel that a change has been long overdue and that now is the time, finally, for linguistics to take account of the criticisms that have been addressed to it (see for example Love 1990 and Baker and Hacker 1984).

Redefining linguistics is an enterprise of a different order from redefining history, or mathematics, or geography, or music. For these subjects, i.e. disciplines, are not open to redefinition in the same sense. Whatever reassessment is made of their contents, the subject itself remains recognizably intact.

Linguistics, however, is different. Some linguists sense the difference, but misconstrue it. According to Crystal, the problem resides in 'the relative newness of the subject' (Crystal 1977: 1). He defines the subject in *A Dictionary of Linguistics and Phonetics* as follows: '**linguistics** The scientific study of language. As an academic discipline, the development of this subject has been recent and rapid, having become particularly widely known and taught in the 1960s' (Crystal 1985: 181). But, even allowing for the historical foreshortening in this account, the mere novelty of a subject can hardly explain the problem its practitioners have in defining what it is they are doing.

The difference between history, mathematics, geography, etc. and linguistics is simple but fundamental. In the case of linguistics the subject is also the subject matter, as Saussure implicitly

1

acknowledged over half a century ago when he identified one of the aims of linguistics as being to 'delimit and define linguistics itself' (Saussure 1922: 20).

Roy Harris points out that for Saussure a definition of the term *linguistics* as the designation of a given form of inquiry 'would have been incongruous to say the least, in view of Saussure's forthright and absolute condemnation of nomenclaturism' (Harris 1987a: 11). Whether Saussure in fact actually understood the relevance and force of his statement is beyond the scope of this paper. What will be considered here are the implications of the thesis that linguistics is to be seen 'as constituting its own subject-matter' (Love: 114 in this volume).

Many linguists have ignored this problem of definition, simply saying 'Linguistics is the science of "language itself" '. This definition has suited scholars, as it has allowed them the prestige of being called 'scientists' (albeit incestuously, for it is only linguists who think of other linguists as scientists). As Harris states, 'the basis of linguistic theory has remained in all essentials unchanged since it was first laid down in Saussure's Geneva lectures of 1907–11' (Harris: 21 in this volume). Harris's explanation for this is the unquestioning acceptance, by modern linguists, of Saussure's two principles of linearity and arbitrariness wedded to a 'telementational' view of communication.

A sceptic may query, 'If linguistics is not to describe languages scientifically, what else can it do?' Such questions in part are due to a perceived disciplinary gap, in that 'linguistics' was rather late on the scene. Other scholars had staked out areas of language study for their own territory (rhetoric, philology, stylistics, dialectology, etc.), leaving an unoccupied space for the study of 'language itself', i.e. for its own sake.

However, what 'language itself' is has by no means been incontrovertible. A quick look at the practice of linguists reveals that there is no consensus about what is or is not part of this object. Moreover, it is often unclear whether linguists are basing their theories on *a* language, such as English, French, Swahili, etc., or on language in the more general sense. Carroll for instance sees linguistics as 'the study of languages conceived as what may be called "linguistic codes" ' (Carroll 1955: 2), a language being:

> a structured system of arbitrary vocal sounds and sequences
> of sounds which is used, or can be used, in interpersonal

communication by an aggregation of human beings, and which rather exhaustively catalogs the things, events, and processes in the human environment.

(Carroll 1955: 10)

This seems, however, to be the definition of *language* according to Bolinger: 'Human language is a system of vocal-auditory communication, interacting with the experiences of its users, employing conventional signs composed of arbitrary patterned sound units' (Bolinger 1981: 2). For Carroll, the linguist is not concerned with psychological aspects of communication; he does not 'inquire into the mechanisms, psychological or otherwise, whereby human beings are able to use linguistic symbols' (Carroll 1955: 12). Rather, 'he is interested primarily in the vehicle of communication, that is, the language system' (1955: 12). For Chomsky however, linguistics is *part of* psychology and he considers a linguistics

which concerns itself solely with the system that is acquired and not with the manner in which it is acquired or in the ways it is put to use confines itself within too narrow limits, and omits the consideration of issues that may have great importance for its narrower goals, which are of great interest in themselves.

(Chomsky 1979: 44)

Linguists' views on the ontogenesis of this language system often determine in part what other aspects of 'communication' are to be subsumed in a linguistic theory and considered thereafter as part of (a) language. Hence Carroll, feeling that 'children learn language behavior quite early in life' (Carroll 1955: 88), excludes semantics from linguistics, adducing the same reasons as Bloomfield (Bloomfield 1935: 139) – to be 'concerned with the content of communication, [the linguist] would in effect be concerned with the totality of human knowledge' (Carroll 1955: 12), and not therefore with the structure of the 'linguistic code' *per se*. Whereas Chomsky, who investigates the cognitive structures in the mind 'organized according to a genetic program that determines their function, their structure, the process of their development' and whose realization depends on some kind of interaction with the environment (Chomsky 1979: 83), realizes that he is compelled at least to acknowledge a distinction between 'linguistic' and 'factual' knowledge but is 'at present' unable to rigorously draw a boundary between the two: 'I doubt that one can separate semantic representation from beliefs and knowledge about the world' (1979: 142). Thus for Chomsky 'only a bare framework of semantic properties, altogether insufficient for characterizing what is ordinarily called "the meaning of a linguistic expression," can be associated correctly with the idealization "language" ' (1979: 143). However Bolinger, who is unsure of the ontogenesis of language ('We do not know the extent to which children are taught and the extent to which they learn on their own' (Bolinger 1981: 165)), considers it important for linguists to fit together 'the partially fixed semantic entities that we carry in our heads, tied to the words and forms of sentences, to approximate the way reality is fitted together as it comes to us from moment to moment' (Bolinger 1981: 109), without feeling compelled to state the ontological status of such 'semantic entities'.

Similarly, there is no more consensus about whether phonetics is or is not part of this object 'language'. Catford concurs with Sweet's view that phonetics is the foundation for language study 'since it expresses well a view which is still current in British linguistics: the importance of a thorough practical and theoretical knowledge of phonetics as the essential basis of all language study' (Catford 1969: 220). Whereas, for Bolinger, only *representations* of sounds, not sounds themselves, are encoded in the brain or mind. So he feels that:

> The science of *phonetics*, whose domain is the sounds of speech, is to linguistics what numismatics is to finance: it makes no difference to a financial transaction what alloys are used in a coin, and it makes no difference to the brain what bits of substance are used as triggers for language.
>
> (Bolinger 1981: 3)

Similarly Chomsky, because he is mainly concerned with the acquisition of a mentally represented rule system which enables one to become a fully competent language-user, considers what is traditionally known as 'sociolinguistics' as irrelevant to any linguistic theory:

> Sociolinguistics is, I suppose, a discipline that seeks to apply principles of sociology to the study of language; but I suspect that it can draw little from sociology, and I wonder whether it is likely to contribute much to it . . . You can also collect

butterflies and make many observations. If you like butterflies, that's fine; but such work must not be confounded
with research.

(Chomsky 1979: 57)

Labov, however, feels that the term 'sociolinguistics' is redun-
dant since there cannot be a 'successful linguistic theory or practice
which is not social' (Labov 1972: xiii). As he does not want to
abolish the notion of a static rule system completely (Chomsky's
'competence'), he introduces 'variable rules' thereby incorporating
certain aspects of linguistic variation 'by fiat into the static model'
(Bailey and Harris 1985: x).

In effect, this introduced a radically new descriptive concept
of a language, inasmuch as *the speakers (or certain facts about the
speakers) were now treated as part of the system*, whereas previously
the system had been an independent abstraction, having only
a contingent connexion with any particular community of
users and their social life.

All this should indicate that linguistics is not a subject with a
clearly (if at all) defined subject-matter. In most other disciplines
the subject-matter precedes the subject. The lack of consensus on
what language, or a language, is in itself shows that this has not
been the case with linguistics. Thus, the first reason for a
redefinition of linguistics is a negative one; how can one have a
scientific study of an ill-defined entity? The positive reason for a
redefinition is to show that there are and always will be endless
redefinitions.

Despite such differences of opinion, all the linguists mentioned
believe that somehow their language system consists of linguistic
units, relations, and combinations that are, at some level of
description, determinate. If language were not determinate, then it
would leave three questions unanswered: (i) how could communication work? (ii) how could linguistics be a science? (iii) how
could writing be such an accurate representation of language?

Communication works, according to traditional linguists, because all speakers of the 'same' language share the same
correlations of forms with meanings. For example if A wishes to
convey the idea 'I like tea' to B, he or she will utter the forms
corresponding to the individual meanings of 'I', 'like', and 'tea'. B
in turn will understand such an utterance because he or she will

5

have the same series of forms corresponding to the same series of meanings. A corollary of this point is that without such a series of determinate units, there could be no science of language because there could be no way of *systematically* analysing language. As Harris says:

> If we define speech as oral communication, and communication as telementation [i.e. thought transference], then the task of linguistics is to provide a theoretical framework for explaining what makes speech possible and how it may be systematically analyzed. Given that we cannot discover any natural principles which explain how the forms of speech are determined by their meanings, then the simplest hypothesis would be that speaker and hearer share a fixed code of arbitrary signs, in which determinate meanings attach to determinate discrete segments in the flow of speech.
>
> (Harris: 31 in this volume)

The view that writing is an accurate representation of speech or language lends further appeal to the advocacy of linguistic determinacy:

> Each element (letter or written word) in the system corresponds to a specific element (sound or sound-group or spoken word) in the primary system. Written language is thus a point-to-point equivalence, to borrow a mathematical phrase, to its spoken counterpart.
>
> (Sapir 1921: 19–20)

So it was the invention of writing, and especially printing, that gave linguists the conception of language(s) as a determinate system of units spoken by a 'homogeneous speech community' (Harris 1980, 1981) and that ultimately presented 'grammar' as *a prioristic* instead of an epiphenomenal process of textual structuration. Yet linguists do not consider writing to be part of language. It is seen as unnatural: computers having no linguistic knowledge and therefore unable to engage in telementation can be programmed to produce texts. One can therefore make no scientific discoveries about this invention, precisely because writing itself is an invention. However, in literate societies, writing is very much a part of one's concept of a language; in fact it was writing itself that created the distinction between speech and language (Harris 1983: 15), thus influencing metalinguistic awareness and therefore

6

linguistics. That Saussure's theory is based upon the written word is shown explicitly in his discussion of the linguistic sign which has a determinate form and meaning. And in order to identify the signs in the way therein described (Saussure 1922: 146) it is necessary to give priority to the 'signifiants', for by what other means would Saussure be able to say that the French 'au' was a single sign? He certainly could not say that it was composed of two signs. His alphabetic bias is further shown in his description of the sign as having a linear nature, i.e. composed of a linear chain of sounds.

Thus, although not being able to dispense with or ignore writing completely, theorists end up relegating it to a mere representation of speech or language, a view challenged by Love and Harris in the following papers. We are therefore presented with a linguistics which treats, as Culler claims, the 'norm of language' as 'an ideal associated with speech' (Culler 1987: 177). He envisages a 'linguistics of writing' in order to give 'a central place to those aspects of language set aside by this [idealised] model, whether they are associated with the written character or with features of speech neglected by linguistic idealisation' (Culler 1987: 177). A linguistics of writing, according to Culler, would show that many linguistic effects are produced

> that do not seem to involve linguistic conventions at all, as in the sound patterning of advertising slogans or of poetry, which may do its work without a reader or listener becoming explicitly aware of it. Either way, the model of language as a system of signs seems under attack.
>
> (Culler 1987: 179–80)

The orthodox theorists, in their endeavour to make language a scientific object of inquiry, therefore posit an idealized, abstract system – a 'fixed code' – in order to explain how language makes communication possible. As the papers in this volume show, the explanatory power of this idealization is zero. Harris demonstrates that the postulation of a fixed code rules out the possibility both of innovation in language, and of learning a new word. For A to ask B the meaning of a word would lead to 'a paradox of inquiry' in that if A and B have the same fixed code, then A must already know the meaning of the word; whereas if they have different codes then, being *fixed* codes, A can never come to understand the meaning of this new word by asking B. However, if B can introduce a new word that A will understand, then the code cannot have been fixed.

For Taylor, this determinacy thesis comes under attack by excluding the moral, political, and cultural aspects of language. These aspects are fundamental to a linguistic theory, for it is the normativity of language which explains why language is the sort of patterned behaviour that it is.

For Hopper, language cannot be determinate, for language is not something that *is*, rather it is always something that is *emergent*. It is a real-time, social, and temporal phenomenon. As his study of proper names shows, the 'structure' of language is not something rigidly fixed, but rather is provisional and negotiable in both monologic and polyadic discourse.

One of Love's objections to linguistic determinacy is that it is unclear how this 'fixed-code' could have been phylogenetically established. For when primordial A first spoke and B understood, there was no possibility of their having come to any prior agreement on linguistic units; neither, therefore, could their understanding have arisen by means of antecedently given units. 'The first utterance logically cannot have been the utterance *of* something antecedently given' (Love: 107 in this volume).

Furthermore, under this theory of language, *every* word would have to have a determinate form and meaning. If this were so one would have a problem not only in characterizing various meanings, but also in locating various forms. It is unclear that 'to', for example, has a fixed meaning or set of meanings, and what these meanings actually are. To take three simple sentences: (a) I want to eat; (b) Ten to six; (c) I went to the shops; all speakers of the 'same' fixed code would have to *at least* agree as to whether the instances of 'to' are the same or different. If A thinks that (a) and (b) are the same, whereas B thinks that (a) and (c) are the same, then they are obviously not sharing the same fixed-code. Identifying fixed forms in speech is no easier, as in the problem of trying to locate 'is' in utterances of the following types: [ɪnɪt] (isn't it), [eynt] (aint), [snat fɛr] (it's not fair).

Thus there can be no determinate *object* for linguistics to be a science of. The definition of linguistics as the 'science of language' collapses, and a redefinition is in order.

Saussure was at least right in arguing that any search for an object of linguistic study will be fruitless. The only perspective from which he considered language should or can be studied is that of the ordinary language-user, i.e. from a *subjective* perspective, from which environmental 'objects' are made linguistically pertinent.

(As Harris says elsewhere, 'The language-user already has the only concept of a language worth having' (Harris 1980: 3).) Saussure's mistake, of course, was in assuming that this significance-determining-perspective is shared by all members of the same community in all situations. This assumption created the structuralist's problem of circumscribing the community, a problem finally leading to Chomsky's 'resolution' in speaking of an ideal, individual, speaker-hearer.

However, if one takes the insider's view of language, the first thing that will become apparent is that such a view yields no determinate entity since it is not itself determinate. Such a view will vary from speaker to speaker, situation to situation, purpose to purpose, etc. Moreover, language is a creative process: as Hopper says, it is always in the process of being made, always 'emerging', never stable. Wilhelm von Humboldt seems to have anticipated this view of language with his distinction between *energeia*, language as 'a doing', and *ergon*, language as something done. Thus for Humboldt 'Language is *always* "an act, a truly creative performance of the mind", and an act performed by an individual with freedom of the will' (Harris and Taylor 1989: 156).

The context of the linguistic act, which includes the assumptions the speaker may hold about the hearer's intentions, thus creates the sign. The linguistic sign is not given in advance of the situation. This being so, language is necessarily influenced by what orthodox linguists call the 'extra-linguistic' – knowledge of the world, contextual knowledge, power relationships, memory limitations, drunkenness . . . . Therefore, being 'integrational', there can be no autonomy in a redefined linguistics.

So because language is a human activity which, like all other human activities, influences and is influenced by social and political norms, it is irredeemably ideological. To treat it as if it were not is simply to impose a particular ideology. This is a point rarely acknowledged by traditional linguists, sometimes even denied. 'What special knowledge I have concerning language has no immediate bearing on social and political issues' (Chomsky 1979: 3). This remark is especially disturbing given the context in which it is written, a recorded interview on Chomsky's political and linguistic views in which Chomsky's method of 'debunking' political analysis seems to more or less concur with the criticisms of traditional linguistic inquiry presented in this collection of papers. He says:

For the analysis of ideology, which occupies me very much, a bit of open-mindedness, normal intelligence, and healthy skepticism will generally suffice.

(Chomsky 1979: 3)

With a little industry and application, anyone who is willing to extricate himself from the system of shared ideology and propaganda will readily see through the modes of distortion developed by substantial segments of the intelligentsia.

(Chomsky 1979: 4)

If such analysis is often carried out poorly, that is because, quite commonly, social and political analysis is produced to defend special interests rather than to account for the actual events.

(Chomsky 1979: 4)

Although Chomsky does not recognize it linguistics thus seems to be in a similar position to political analysis in that academic linguistics cannot help but reflect and reproduce the prejudices, preconceptions, and ideologies of our culture (Taylor: 146 in this volume).

Topics such as racism, sexism, and obscenity, for example, which necessarily involve one's use of language, cannot be investigated from an objective standpoint because they are personal issues bound up with ideology. Treating language as a purely objective fact existing independently of intentions, evaluations, or usages, cannot explain why we have taboos on certain words. Article 12 from the Policies of the Board of Governors at Northeast Missouri State University, states that a student can be expelled from campus for the 'use of vulgar, obscene or profane language'. As all these are evaluative, i.e. subjective, terms the orthodox linguist has no basis for investigating this statement.

In his *Invitation to Linguistics*, one of Hudson's mentioned 'job-descriptions' for the linguist is to improve the vocabulary of English, mentioning by way of example the elimination of sexist terms (Hudson 1984: 156). But likewise, he would be unable to offer any assistance to the feminist who bemoans the use of sexist language: for the linguist, 'sexist' is a subjective term. But the categories 'sexist language' and 'obscene language' are considered to be applied to all manifestations of a single token. For instance the use of 'fuck', and 'chairman' no matter who is uttering these words, i.e. divorced from any situation, are considered respectively

10

'obscene' and 'sexist'. However as has been demonstrated elsewhere, 'sexist language' is not a linguistic category amenable to formal identification, but rather an analytic category of one's individual linguistic experience (Davis 1989).

Only by thus taking account of what matters to the ordinary speaker-hearer in their determination of what is communicationally relevant in the speech event can linguistics, as a professional perspective on language, be made sense of to the layman. To tell the layman (as orthodox linguistics does) that what he or she does care about in language is not in fact linguistically pertinent, is to manufacture a linguistics which, although secure within a tiny niche of the academic institution, *is not itself pertinent*. Crystal's introductory textbook *What is Linguistics?* demonstrates how far removed orthodox linguistics is from the lay perspective. He begins by saying 'a relatively complete survey of Linguistics is far too ambitious for one's first reading in the subject' (Crystal 1977: 2):

> Linguists tend to forget the great gap which exists between their study of language and the views of the man in the street. They often take too much for granted, introduce technical terms with too little explanation, or focus their attention on relatively specialist or restricted areas of study.
>
> (Crystal 1977: 3)

Given Chomsky's clear-sightedness in respect of political theorizing, it is thus somewhat paradoxical to see that the desperate need for a redefinition of linguistics is largely due to his own linguistic theorizing. He declares linguistics to be a branch of psychology concentrating on 'the language faculty':

> What we loosely call "knowledge of language" involves in the first place knowledge of grammar – indeed, that language is a derivative and perhaps not very interesting concept – and beyond that other cognitive systems that interact with grammar: conceptual systems with their specific properties and organizing principles may be quite different in character from the "computational" language faculty; pragmatic competence might be a cognitive system distinct and differently structured from grammatical competence; these systems may furthermore be composed of distinct though interacting components.
>
> (Chomsky 1980: 90)

11

This grammar which is represented in the mind is, according to Chomsky, a 'real object' by which a person's language can be defined (Chomsky 1980: 120). 'I would like to suggest that in certain fundamental respects we do not really learn language; rather, grammar grows in the mind' (Chomsky 1980: 134).

To insist that linguistics is mainly concerned with the acquisition of some mentally represented rule system is to rule out of consideration everything that shows that 'language matters', and that it has effects on freedom of speech and publication, no less than religion and creed. The publication of Salman Rushdie's book *The Satanic Verses* is a case in point. This book received extensive world-wide publicity, led to riots, deaths, and death threats, and has caused the author to go into hiding. The controversy stems from the fact that the Muslim community consider the book to be blasphemous and ridiculing Islam. Rushdie claims that *The Satanic Verses* is a work of fiction. Nevertheless the late Ayatollah Khomeini was reported to have sentenced Rushdie, *and his publishers* to death:

'I ask all the Muslims to execute them wherever they find them,' he was quoted as saying.

He said that if the attackers were killed carrying out his order to execute Salman Rushdie and his collaborators, they would be considered martyrs.

(*South China Morning Post* 15 February 1989)

Muslims later demonstrated in Pakistan, leading to six deaths. In response to this situation, Rushdie was quoted in the same article as saying 'The book that is worth killing people for and burning flags for is not the book that I wrote. The people who demonstrated in Pakistan and who were killed haven't read the book because it isn't on sale there'. According to Benazir Bhutto, the Prime Minister of Pakistan, the demonstrations may not have been against the book, but rather the book may have been used as a 'pretext by those who lost the election to try and destabilise the process of democracy'.

This controversy cannot be resolved by any objective analysis. Crystal feels that a qualified linguist is able to resolve problems of interpretation by carrying out 'some kind of analysis of what the text actually says' (Crystal 1977: 67). But in this case, and every such case, the text 'will say' different things to different people in different situations, depending on one's system of beliefs and ideology. Problems of interpretation *cannot* be resolved by staring

12

hard at any piece of writing or listening intently to any utterance. If A thinks that a policy which states 'gambling for money or property is forbidden on campus' does not include IOUs whereas B thinks it does, no amount of linguistic analysis will be able to resolve the issue, no matter how many dictionaries and grammars are at hand. Similarly, no linguist, *pace* Crystal, can 'rationalize the subjectivity' inherent in a person's like or dislike for a poem by 'looking at the language' (Crystal 1977: 77).

To claim, as Chomsky does, that these sorts of issues are of little interest to the linguist is to ignore the importance language plays in one's life.

Moreover, even *if* one were to accept the determinacy fallacy, the purpose and applications of orthodox linguistics remain unclear. Because such linguists ignore the individual's perspective on language, they cannot address any relevant, pertinent, or interesting questions, as most introductory textbooks on the subject demonstrate. David Crystal's *What is Linguistics?* clearly, concisely, and unintentionally makes clear all the pitfalls that confront present-day linguists. It speaks of a linguist as a scientific discoverer who needs years of training to understand this mysterious object called 'language'. Crystal feels free to claim that 'many people see the word "Linguistics", and assume that they know what it means, while in fact they do not' (Crystal 1977: 4). This is a rather strange claim given the fact that linguists do not agree upon definitions and objects of study.

Crystal's sentiments were voiced ten years earlier in Hughes' *The Science of Language*:

> [until recently, at least,] nobody has thought about language. Also, everybody has thought himself an authority on all linguistic matters, which exemplifies another axiom: where there is not – or is not known to be – a formal science of a subject, everyone regards himself as entitled to an opinion, however ill-founded or irrational it might be. Where there are no scientists, there are no laymen.
>
> (Hughes 1967: 3)

He states that there is now a new body of scientists, called 'linguists', who study what language is and how it works, replacing 'wives tales' with a body of experimentally established facts about this most vital of human activities and who have finally answered questions about it that for a thousand centuries had been asked

13

without receiving serious, well-founded or proven answers (Hughes 1967: 3–4).

What is missing from these, and all such accounts, is how linguists eventually discerned their true object of study; how and why the change occurred from wives' tale anecdotes to 'objective', 'descriptive', and 'general' statements. Linguists' pronouncements upon the subject do not offer any help. Crystal, for instance, only tells us what linguistics is when he has finished his discussion of what it is not. But to approach linguistics in this way is to ignore the subjective perspective and therefore the problem of definition – that linguistics is to be seen as constituting its own subject-matter. What is not linguistically relevant to one person may be extremely pertinent to another. Crystal says that:

> Linguistics performs at least two tasks: it is concerned with the study of particular languages as ends in themselves, in order to be able to produce complete and accurate descriptions of them; and it also studies languages as a means to a further end, in order to be able to obtain information about the nature of language in general . . . [The linguist] tries to be as objective as possible, and aims to avoid the misconceptions about the nature of language and languages which have been so dominant.
>
> (Crystal 1977: 26)

To what extent one can be objective and avoid misconceptions in a linguistic analysis Crystal does not think worth discussing. In endeavouring to answer the question 'how do we describe a language scientifically?', he dismisses the lay answer 'everyone knows what a language is' as a misconception fostered by our upbringing and 'a contempt bred by our familiarity with language' (Crystal 1977: 29). 'Language, like all other skills, does not come naturally; . . . we tend to take it for granted – until, of course, something starts to go wrong' (Crystal 1977: 29).

Again, what the 'it' is, is a point brushed aside. We are only told 'Language, to put it mildly, is a very complex phenomenon' (Crystal 1977: 30). A linguist merely concentrates on phonetics, phonology, and grammar in a factual, objective manner.

The reasons adduced in introductory textbooks for studying linguistics are rather unenlightening. Hudson's first statement upon this issue is telling in its negative sentiment: 'Apart from a career as an academic linguist (which I haven't even bothered to list as there are so few professional openings), there are no careers for which a degree in linguistics would be a specific training' (Hudson 1984: 152). First on Crystal's list of reasons for embarking upon such a study is earning a degree. Second is the possibility of doing research, and third is the need for trained linguists in non-linguistic fields. For Crystal these fields include education, psychology, sociology, and computational work. However, one of the strongest reasons for pursuing this field is in the area of applied linguistics – language teaching, or speech pathology, or machine translation. He finally lists a series of jobs ranging from working in the Civil Service to a 'department store'.

But, focusing on the reference to language teaching as a job opportunity for linguists, it is worth considering a book written by Lindemann in which there is a chapter entitled 'What do teachers need to know about linguistics?' (Lindemann 1982: 93). This was written to improve students' writing skills and:

> to examine the role language plays in the composing process, especially at the writing and rewriting stages. That is when students are principally concerned with manipulating language, putting ideas into words and examining the words to determine if they express ideas effectively. The more we know about how English works, the more linguistic options we can suggest to students struggling to get the words right.
>
> (Lindemann 1982: 93)

She claims that there are many misconceptions about language which can be sorted out by linguists. She draws a distinction between grammar, one's 'intuitive knowledge of language', one's 'capacity for language', and usage, referring 'to linguistic etiquette, to socially sanctioned styles of language appropriate to given situations and audiences' (Lindemann 1982: 99). This, however, begs the question of how we can have knowledge of or capacity for language without any reference to etiquette, situations, or audiences. Of what does this capacity consist without all the above? The only 'facts' worth knowing in the assessment of good writing is who is writing to whom and for what purpose.

Crystal endorses Lindemann with his statements on what linguistics is not. According to Crystal it is not the study of the history of language, of the learning of languages, of literary criticism, or other fields involving a scale of values, such as speech training, or of traditional grammar. Such statements are rather

15

perplexing given Crystal's discussion of the uses and applications of linguistics. If one wishes to divorce language from history, how does one propose to analyse the relationship between language and literature, or to discover whether all languages have the same parts of speech? For when considered ahistorically a language has no basis for comparison. To make sense of Chaucerian or Shake-spearean English, for example, one needs to situate it within its historical context, i.e. have some sort of notion of when it was written, otherwise it could be seen as just nonsense.

Similarly, in his discussion of why linguistics is not concerned with language learning or teaching, he is open to the same criticism as Lindemann. Crystal writes:

> When the linguist looks at language in use, he is simply concerned with describing the facts of the utterances, to see what patterns of sound, grammar and vocabulary are being used . . . he is not trying to evaluate the language in terms of some aesthetic, moral, or other critical standard.
>
> (Crystal 1977: 8)

Yet how can we begin to study language unless it is being used, either verbally or orthographically? And when it is being used, how can we divorce from it morals, opinions, or evaluations?

This viewpoint of objectivity has been adopted purely for disciplinary reasons, to make linguistics an autonomous science. How this is to be achieved depends on the viewpoint of the theorist. As mentioned previously, it is unclear what the object of the linguist's investigation actually is, and it is certainly clear that language cannot be demarcated, let alone objectified. The methods of linguists have lent support to and been supported by other disciplines, social practices, and attitudes. But they find little support in everyday linguistic experience.

The primary goal of a redefinition of linguistics should be to demonstrate that language is not an objective matter. To say that one must study language objectively is to say that one must study human behaviour and everything that goes with it – intentionality, morality, sexual and emotional activity – objectively. But where the criteria of objectivity are to come from remains unexplained in these cases.

Linguistics is, and should be, the study of whatever is linguistically pertinent. And this, as a mode of inquiry, can be assessed independently of the thesis therein set out. A discussion of grammar for example may under certain circumstances be extremely linguistically pertinent, but to claim that the study of grammar can divulge some fundamental 'truth' about the workings of language is to confound mythologies with truths. On the other hand it could be revealing and pertinent for the linguist to investigate the source and role of such mythologies (see Harris 1980).

Rather than strive for a mythical objectivity a linguistics redefined would look at how we interpret and construct our day-to-day communication acts, what views of language are shared by and opposed by societies, and the source and roles that these views play in our living and learning experience. The following papers argue the case for such a redefinition more explicitly than has ever been done before in modern linguistic theory. Such a redefined perspective, precisely because it is a perspective, subject to 'outside' influence, and in constant dialogue with the perspective of the other human sciences, must be endlessly redefined. Thus, although linguistics is unregulated ('the game we play with it is unregulated' (Wittgenstein 1953: para. 68)), it can never be redefined out of existence – only into existence, into an analytic understanding of one's individual linguistic experience.

Versions of the following papers were read at the 'Linguistics Redefined' conference in March 1989, held at Northeast Missouri State University, Kirksville. We would like to thank all the participants for their stimulating and lively discussions. Our special thanks go to President McClain, the university administration, and to the students of Ryle North College, all of whom supported and sponsored the conference. Without their assistance this book probably would never have been published.

The editors would also like to thank Kate Renko and David Morrill for editorial assistance.

The editors, on behalf of all those who participated in the conference, would like to express a special thanks to Roy Harris. By his writing and teaching he has inspired many to an interest in linguistics; without him neither the conference nor this book would ever have been realized.

2

ON REDEFINING
LINGUISTICS

Roy Harris

INTRODUCTION

An American philosopher once wrote of Renoir's painting:

> The nudes of Renoir give us delight with no pornographic
> suggestion. The voluptuous qualities of flesh are retained,
> even accentuated. But conditions of the physical existence of
> nude bodies have been abstracted from. Through abstrac-
> tion and by means of the medium of color, ordinary
> associations with bare bodies are transferred into a new
> realm, for these associations are practical stimuli which
> disappear in the work of art. The esthetic repeals the
> physical, and the heightening of qualities common to flesh
> with flowers ejects the erotic. The conception that objects
> have fixed and unalterable values is precisely the prejudice
> from which art emancipates us.
>
> (Dewey 1934: 95)

The descriptive linguist, if we are to believe some accounts, is a
Renoir operating in the field of speech. What the linguist's
descriptions show us is language stripped of its mundane values,
but accentuating its bare essentials: language unclothed, but
divested too of the 'practical stimuli' which would ordinarily
accompany it. Such a description leaves us free to delight in the
aesthetics of language structure, its symmetries and complexities,
purified of any plebeian communicational interpretations.

It might perhaps be objected to the view of Renoir quoted above
that it reduces Renoir's nudes to examples of still life. He might
just as well have painted pineapples: the philosopher's comments,

if they are valid, would still apply. And much the same objection carries over to the parallel account of linguistic description. But at least Renoir never claimed to be giving a scientific account of the female body; whereas the linguist commonly claims to be giving a scientific account of the structure of speech. Perhaps, on the other hand, a linguist would insist that the conception of speech as merely a chain of physical events is precisely the prejudice from which linguistics emancipates us. But what the philosopher does not sufficiently allow for is that our view of Renoir may depend on our own definition of painting. And that applies equally in the case of language.

THE RISE OF LINGUISTICS

Like painting, language may be viewed – and has been viewed – in different ways at different times in history. Since the end of the eighteenth century, two radical changes of perspective have taken place in language studies in the western intellectual world.

The first of these changes accompanied the establishment of linguistics itself as an independent branch of inquiry in the early decades of the nineteenth century. This came about when scholars began to realize that relationships between languages could be studied as a subject in its own right. The term 'linguistique' was admitted to the dictionary of the French Academy in 1835 and there defined as 'the study of the principles and relationships of languages'. But the new discipline was also known as 'comparative grammar', a term proposed by Schlegel in 1808; and that is the designation which perhaps described better than any other the new orientation of linguistic scholarship. Prompted by the rediscovery of Sanskrit, European linguists embarked on the comparative analysis of the whole family of Indo-European languages. This marked a clear break with the academic grammatical and philological studies of the previous century, which had been directed primarily towards commentary on and elucidation of important ancient texts. Comparative grammar brought to light many resemblances between the various Indo-European languages. Seeking historical reasons for these resemblances, linguists were inevitably led to attempt to reconstruct the linguistic developments which had given rise to them. Thus by the end of the century, linguistics had become a branch of scholarship defined by its focus on the history of related languages.

The second major change of perspective, and the first redefinition of linguistics itself, came at the beginning of the present century. It was associated primarily with the revolution in linguistic theory ushered in by the work of the Geneva school, led by Saussure. Its effect was to redirect attention away from the history of languages towards the analysis of the synchronic linguistic system, considered as a subject of study in its own right, irrespective of its antecedents and irrespective of its relationship to other such systems. Redefining linguistics in this way gave the discipline the essential academic profile which it has retained down to the present day.

The Geneva school structuralists conceived linguistics as a science of speech communication based on two theoretical principles. These two principles were called the 'principle of arbitrariness' and the 'principle of linearity'. Their adoption resulted in a linguistics which investigated the human language faculty at one remove; that is to say, not directly through the analysis of particular linguistic acts, but indirectly through the analysis of postulated systems underlying them. It was for these postulated systems that Saussure reserved the term *'langue'*. Each such language (*langue*) was envisaged as an independent, self-contained object of knowledge, known to its users. In each such system the minimum linguistic sign consisted of a string of one or more phonemes, associated with a given meaning, and sentences consisted of strings of such signs meaningfully arranged in syntagmatic combinations.

Today this is still the portrayal of speech communication which linguistics offers its students. Writing is discounted as a mere second-order representation of speech, and speech is defined, implicitly or explicitly, as the use by individuals or communities of oral systems of the type just described. It is a remarkable fact that no major school of twentieth-century linguistics – structuralists, distributionalists, glossematicians, generativists, tagmemicists, or stratificationalists – ever, as a school, renounced Saussure's twin principles. No major linguistic theorist ever called them in question. Even those who refused to subscribe to the bi-planarity of the linguistic sign did not query arbitrariness or linearity. This is not to say that these two basic principles were never the subject of attack or controversy. Nevertheless, in spite of the divisions and changes of emphasis that have marked the development of linguistics throughout this century, the basis of linguistic theory has remained in all essentials unchanged since it was first laid down in Saussure's Geneva lectures of 1907–1911.

Whether or not we agree with Saussure's view of language, that is the ultimate testimonial to his theoretical acumen. He redefined linguistics in such a way that even those who disagreed with him were forced to accept that definition, and work within it or around it. Any new redefinition, therefore, is still an enterprise – if anyone wishes to attempt it – which must begin from the original Saussurean thesis. The task is itself defined by reference to that theoretical position, which has dominated the academic study of language for most of the present century.

It has also dominated the view of language taken in neighbouring disciplines, where it was welcome because it relieved those disciplines of the burden of undertaking their own linguistic investigations, while allowing them to make use of results obtained in linguistics. If linguistics was a science, as the Geneva school claimed, then all empirical linguistic questions could safely be passed on to the linguist for an expert answer. Furthermore, by implicitly limiting the range of questions the linguist was competent to handle, the orthodox view did not threaten any encroachment upon the academic territory of others. The result was to establish a division of labour in which the field of linguistics was demarcated from such adjacent fields as anthropology, sociology, psychology, physiology, philosophy, and literary studies, all of which claimed some professional interest in language. This whole division of labour rested on the premiss that a viable definition of linguistics had been reached and had been provided with a sound theoretical foundation.

What in fact that definition amounted to was a decision to restrict the concept 'language' in a particularly narrow way. In the first place, it restricted language to speech; and then it restricted speech to the production of determinate strings of phonemes, segmentable into determinate substrings, each identifiable as the manifestation of a determinate linguistic sign. Each linguistic sign was assumed to have a determinate form, a determinate meaning, and a determinate capacity for linear combination with other linguistic signs. In brief, it was a linguistics which could handle the phenomena of speech only in so far as a speaker's vocalization was reducible to a set of determinate phonological forms with determinate meanings and a determinate combinatorial pattern. Any aspects of speech not reducible to this schema were simply ignored.

The basic contention of the present paper is that the fundamental error in contemporary linguistics is still the fundamental error of Saussure's original thesis. It involves a crude process of abstraction by which certain phenomena are segregated from the continuum of human communication, and these segregated phenomena are then, rather capriciously, set up for academic purposes as constituting the *linguistic* part of communication.

The mistake, in other words, was already inherent in Saussure's first theoretical move, which was to segregate manifestations of language from all forms of non-linguistic communication by the exclusive identification of the former with signals contained in the auditory flow of speech. This single stroke of Saussure's segregational axe simultaneously separated language from non-language and linguistics from all other investigations dealing with human behaviour. Modern linguistics proceeded to demonstrate its indebtedness to Saussure by remaining profoundly segregationalist both in its methodology and in its attitude to neighbouring disciplines. It conceived its own scientific brief in narrowly segregationalist terms, and accordingly took its primary objective to be the construction of an internal systematics of relationships between units identifiable exclusively within the flow of speech.

The expression 'speech communication' thus acquired an interesting ambiguity. For the lay person it continued to mean simply communication by means of verbal utterances, as distinct from communication by writing, by gestures, or by other means. For the academic linguist, on the other hand, it meant communication restricted to the processes of *parole* as identified by Saussure, a far narrower interpretation. This ambiguity itself worked in favour of the establishment of a linguistic orthodoxy which represented the latter as giving a scientific account of the former.

LESSONS FROM THE 'HISTORY OF LINGUISTICS'

The proclamation of linguistics as a new 'science' did not long precede the date of Saussure's birth. His generation was the first to be brought up on this notion, and he was the first of his generation to address seriously the question of how linguists could produce a theoretical validation of that claim. As is well known, Saussure

22

rejected the academically accepted view of his day, which assumed that linguistics could be founded on the empirical discovery of laws of linguistic evolution, including the famous laws of 'sound change' for the Indo-European languages, discovered in the nineteenth century.

However, once a new 'science' is proclaimed, it inevitably and immediately acquires a history. Its birth is seen as the outcome of earlier views, which are retrospectively resurrected as progenitors. Thus it was with linguistics. Once a subject has retrospectively acquired a history, its practitioners are expected to situate their own practice by reference to it. Thus, again, it was with linguistics. And Saussure, having marked a turning point in that history, automatically validated it. 'Pre-Saussurean' came to be both a chronological and a doctrinal designation; rather like the more familiar expression 'BC'. *Anno Domini* for modern linguistics is established by the date of publication of Saussure's *Cours de linguistique générale*.

Once an orthodoxy is set up, those who are dissatisfied have only two choices. They can seek to set up a privileged version of that orthodoxy; or they can become heretics. This process operates in linguistics in much the same way as in religion, politics, philosophy, and other areas of human endeavour which require an explicit statement of beliefs. But not all self-proclaimed heretics are sufficiently heretical to acquire historical title to that status. Furthermore, heresy may often take the form of claiming to be more strictly orthodox than the orthodox.

It is interesting to reflect that those linguists who, at one time or another, appeared to be offering the most serious theoretical objections to Saussure in the end turned out to be offering no challenge at all. One thinks particularly here of two major figures in American linguistics: Leonard Bloomfield and Zellig Harris. Both, interestingly enough, thought they were redefining linguistics because they held certain views about the nature of science and about the human mind. And indeed they disagreed fundamentally with Saussure both on philosophy of science and on philosophy of psychology. But in retrospect it became clear that disagreeing with Saussure either about the way the human mind works, or about the goals and methods of scientific inquiry, was not in the end going to make much difference to academic linguistics. These were marginal considerations, not central ones; and Saussure would doubtless have been amused had he been able to witness the theoretical posturings of American linguistics during the 1930s and 1940s. By the late 1950s, when at last his posthumous treatise had been translated – or mistranslated – into English, Saussurean views were beginning to appear more congenial to a new generation of American linguists, particularly in so far as those views related to semantics. For it is fundamental to Saussurean thinking that the linguistic sign cannot be defined without reference to what it means. And both Leonard Bloomfield and Zellig Harris had presumed to emphasize the study of formal structures at the expense of the study of linguistic meaning.

It is ironic that Bloomfield in particular never learnt the lessons explicitly drawn in his own criticisms of Saussure. In his review of Saussure's posthumous work in the early 1920s Bloomfield accused Saussure of having 'no psychology beyond the crudest popular notions, and his phonetics are an abstraction from French and Swiss-German which will not stand even the test of an application to English' (Bloomfield 1923: 64). Saussure, therefore, for Bloomfield, scores zero both in psychology and in phonetics. Nevertheless, in the same review, Bloomfield bestows on Saussure the highest of academic accolades. Saussure, says Bloomfield, 'has given us the theoretical basis for a science of human speech' (1923: 65). How is that possible, if Saussure is an ignoramus as regards both phonetics and psychology? For do not sounds and their meanings jointly exhaust the domain of human speech? Bloomfield answers his own conundrum as follows, and thereby defines his own theoretical position. Saussure, he says, 'exemplifies in his own person and perhaps unintentionally, what he proves intentionally and in all due form: that psychology and phonetics do not matter at all and are, in principle, irrelevant to the study of language' (1923: 64). The autonomy of linguistics has not often been asserted more trenchantly.

Ten years later, Bloomfield had become a convert to a then fashionable behaviourism, and gives Saussure only a passing mention on page 19 of his book *Language*, the *magnum opus* of Bloomfieldian linguistics. By that time Bloomfield could not afford to admit that in the study of language psychological theories were irrelevant. So Saussure had to be demoted.

Under Bloomfield's leadership, linguistics in America became even more adamantly segregationalist than the European variety. For the Geneva school, the speech circuit had always included a conceptual component. But for Bloomfield and his followers the only speech phenomena which the linguist could deal with scientifically were those physically present in the articulation of a vocal utterance. Concepts or meanings were not present in this sense, and thus were excluded. In this way the segregation of language from non-language came to be interpreted for all practical purposes as the segregation of the audible sound sequence from everything else.

Where the behaviourists went wrong – wrong, that is to say, had they wished seriously to undermine Saussure's concept of linguistics – was that they accepted as harmless, and even necessary, Saussure's celebrated distinction between synchronic and diachronic linguistics. They misinterpreted this distinction, or at least Bloomfield did; but that is not the point. The point is that once Saussure is allowed his distinction between synchronic and diachronic – however innocuous that concession may seem – then it will be found at the end of the day that the only trump card there was to play against Saussure's game has already been thrown away. It is no good then to take issue on psychological questions. For such questions are already involved in – and presupposed by – the distinction between synchronic and diachronic. That is what Bloomfield failed to see.

A later transatlantic challenge which collapsed was that of transformational-generative grammar. What at first appeared to be novel and un-Saussurean about this approach was its emphasis on algorithmic procedures, an emphasis borrowed from mathematical logic and boosted by the advent of computer-age technology. But this apparent novelty turned out to be merely superficial. Its tacit basis was still the Saussurean linguistic sign, a given string of phonemes with a fixed meaning. Grammar, for the generativists, was a system of relations between forms and meanings, and speech a set of operations by which those systemic relations gave rise to sequences of uttered sounds. Once it was realized that stating the grammar of a language as a set of generative rules is simply one possible formalization of Saussurean syntagmatics, the generativist bid to redefine linguistics faded. Heresy was overnight transformed into orthodoxy. Generativism simply became the currently fashionable framework within which to pursue an analysis of language which was still based on the principles of arbitrariness and linearity, and remained as exclusively segregationalist as Saussure's.

This particular chapter in the history of ideas therefore suggests a useful maxim for those who set up in the business of redefining linguistics. First, make sure you understand why Saussure's principles seem unassailable. If you do not understand that, then your challenge to orthodox twentieth-century linguistics is not only bound to fail, but will be swept along, as those of Bloomfield and others were, in the mainstream of orthodoxy itself.

SPEECH AS A TELEMENTATIONAL PROCESS

These reflections on the history of linguistics lead directly to a key question. Why did the adoption of the principles of arbitrariness and linearity produce a segregationalist linguistics? Was that inevitable? No, it was not inevitable; but it became inevitable once the principle of arbitrariness and the principle of linearity were conjointly wedded to one particular theory of human communication. The theory in question is telementation; that is to say, the theory which explains communication as the transference of thoughts from one person's mind to another person's mind. Saussure adopted telementation as his theory of communication, although he does not designate it by that term. Nevertheless, the adoption is explicitly spelled out in Saussure's account of what he calls the 'speech circuit'.

Saussure's speech circuit envisages the archetypal speech act, reduced to its bare essentials, stripped of all possible ramifications. There are just two participants, A and B, who in turn take on the roles of speaker and hearer. A says something to B, and B in return says something to A. That constitutes one completed lap of the speech circuit. This simple scenario assumes that A and B are speaking the same language. If the only language known by A were Catalan and the only language known by B were Cantonese, this exchange would not constitute a speech circuit in Saussure's sense, regardless of how A and B eked out their oral utterances and their mutual tolerance with gestures, facial expressions and other varieties of non-verbal communication.

Let us suppose, then, for the sake of argument, that A and B are both speaking Kalaba. What happens in the speech circuit, according to Saussure, is that certain ideas occur to A. A wishes to transmit these ideas to B. Because A is a speaker of Kalaba, these ideas trigger in A's mind the phonetic image of certain Kalaba words, which A then proceeds to utter. B hears A's utterance and, being also a speaker of Kalaba, is able to interpret the Kalaba sounds heard as having precisely the meanings which correspond to the original ideas in A's mind, which A intended to transmit to B. Speech communication, on this view, is essentially a process of telementation, or thought-transference. The same thoughts may be transferred from A's mind to B's or from B's mind to A's via exactly the same linguistic procedures; in this case, the procedures laid down by and constitutive of the Kalaba language. So B may then reply to A by using exactly the same sequence of procedures, which will be a selection of those known to both A and B in virtue of their being both speakers of Kalaba.

Before analysing this Saussurean scenario further, it may be as well to offer some documentation of the fact that this still remains the basic scenario which linguists of the present generation endorse. Here are four of the many examples which might have been chosen. (None of these, it should be noted, contains any explicit reference to Saussure. They are presented as simple accounts of self-evident facts about speech communication.)

(1) The first thing the speaker has to do is arrange his thoughts, decide what he wants to say and put what he wants to say into *linguistic form*. The message is put into linguistic form by selecting the right words and phrases to express its meaning, and by placing these words in the correct order required by the grammatical rules of the language. This process is associated with activity in the speaker's brain, and it is in the brain that appropriate instructions, in the form of impulses along the motor nerves, are sent to the muscles of the vocal organs, the tongue, the lips and the vocal cords . . . The movements of the vocal organs generate a speech sound wave that travels through the air between speaker and listener. Pressure changes at the ear activate the listener's hearing mechanism and produce nerve impulses that travel along the acoustic nerve to the listener's brain . . . We see, therefore, that speech communication consists of a chain of events linking the speaker's brain with the listener's brain . . . At the listener's end of the chain, the process is reversed. Events start on a physical level, when the incoming sound wave activates the hearing mechanism. They continue on the physiological level with neural activity in the hearing

27

and perceptual mechanisms. The speech chain is completed on the linguistic level when the listener recognizes the words and sentences transmitted by the speaker.

(Denes and Pinson 1963: 4–7)

(2)   The speaker's message is encoded in the form of a phonetic representation of an utterance by means of the system of linguistic rules with which the speaker is equipped. This encoding then becomes a signal to the speaker's articulatory organs, and he vocalizes an utterance of the proper phonetic shape. This is, in turn, picked up by the hearer's auditory organs. The speech sounds that stimulate these organs are then converted into a neural signal from which a phonetic representation equivalent to the one into which the speaker encoded his message is obtained. This representation is decoded into a representation of the same message that the speaker originally chose to convey by the hearer's equivalent system of linguistic rules.

(Katz 1966: 103–4)

(3)   Language enables a speaker to transform configurations of ideas into configurations of sounds, and it enables a listener within his own mind to transform these sounds back into a reasonable facsimile of the ideas with which the speaker began.

(Chafe 1970: 15)

(4)   *A* has in his head some sort of message (or idea), and he wishes *B* to form in his head the same message. This message is transformed ultimately into a series of neural impulses that are sent to the muscles responsible for the actual production of speech, which follows immediately . . . The listener, *B*, must decode *A*'s message by converting the sounds into a semantic representation.

(Cairns and Cairns 1976: 17–18)

Saussure died in 1913. The four accounts just quoted are in chronological order, and the earliest of the four dates from 1963. Whether these accounts were directly or indirectly influenced by Saussure is not the point. The point is that once any theorist adopts a telementational theory of communication, and attempts to graft on to that theory the principles of arbitrariness and linearity, the inevitable result is that it leaves only one option open for explaining what a language is. The only option open is to construe a language as a fixed code, the fixed code known to both A and B.

LANGUAGES AS FIXED CODES

By a 'fixed code' is meant one which remains invariant from speaker to speaker and from occasion to occasion within the sphere in which it operates. It is fixed in the sense in which the institutionalized rules of a game such as chess are fixed. It is no coincidence that chess was Saussure's favourite analogy for explaining and illustrating how language works. If the rules of chess could change unpredictably during the course of a game or a tournament, then chess would become unplayable. The players would have no guarantee that their moves would bring about the intended results. On the contrary, the results produced might well be the opposite of those intended. But in chess as we understand it, two players are always bound by the same rules, like it or not. The chess code is thus a fixed code, even though different versions of the rules may replace earlier versions in the course of time. It is in a sense exactly analogous to this that when A and B converse in Kalaba, Kalaba is construed as a fixed code.

Why is this theoretically necessary? The answer is that construing a language as a fixed code is demanded by the internal logic of Saussure's speech circuit. Unless the code is fixed, then invoking linguistic knowledge simply does not explain how speech communication works. Given any utterance by A, it is essential that B must not only recognize this utterance as an example of the words A intended to pronounce, but must also attach to those words the same meaning as A does. Otherwise speech communication between A and B necessarily breaks down. This in turn follows from the telementational theory of communication, according to which it is both a necessary and sufficient condition of communication that the ideas which A intends to convey are identical with those which B receives as a result of hearing what A said. Just as in chess, A and B must be following the same rules in order to guarantee that each correctly understands what the other is doing. The fixed code is essential to the concept of a synchronic system. Once change is introduced we are no longer dealing with the original synchronic system but with its diachronic successor.

As in the case of the theory of telementation, Saussure's successors also adopted the theory of the fixed code as a basis for linguistics. This might have been predicted, since the two theories are complementary. The preferred form which the fixed code theory takes in contemporary linguistics involves the postulation of a 'completely homogeneous' speech community. But whether one speaks of fixed codes or completely homogeneous speech communities in the end it amounts to the same thing. The effect in both cases is to eliminate from theoretical consideration the problem of establishing uniformity across individual speakers and communication situations.

To summarize, then, if speech communication is a telemental process, it demands a fixed code which A and B share. If A and B do not share this fixed code, or erroneously suppose they share it when in fact they do not, then speech communication between them must at some point break down, even though the breakdown may not necessarily be obvious to either party, or have pragmatically serious consequences in any particular instance. So the theoretical assumption must be that, somehow or other, those who manage to communicate with each other via speech share and operate a fixed code, even if they do not realize that this is what they are doing. The fixed code is their common language. In this sense, languages take priority over speakers, and over speech: linguistics is thus envisaged as a science primarily concerned, both in general and in particular cases, with analysing languages, which in turn are assumed to be the fixed codes underlying all successful speech communication.

Next let us consider the connection between the postulated fixed code and the twin principles of orthodox linguistics. The relationship is different in the two cases. There is no logical necessity by which a fixed code has to consist of arbitrary signs. But if languages were systems of non-arbitrary signs, then it would become incumbent upon the linguist to identify what natural or causal principles determine the relationships between forms and meanings. In the absence of any identifiable principles of this nature, the only alternative for linguistics is to opt for the thesis that the linguistic sign is arbitrary. However, if the linguistic sign is indeed arbitrary, then it becomes all the more essential to insist that speech communication between A and B depends on A and B using the same fixed code. For, in the absence of natural principles of any kind, there is no *other* way A and B could arrive at identical interpretations of the messages they exchange.

Nor, on the other hand, does a fixed code have to consist of linear signs. But, again, the operation of a fixed code in which signs are arbitrary demands that A and B share some method of identifying individual signs and sign-combinations. The minimal requirement here is to explain how any given complex utterance can be analysed by A and B into its constituent units, on the basis of whatever fixed code is postulated; and the simplest theoretical assumptions to make are that the meanings of individual signs correspond directly to discrete segments of a continuum, and that the continuum has only one dimension. If this continuum is identified with the temporal flow of speech, then it becomes necessary to insist that communication between A and B depends on their knowing how to segment linear sequences of sounds into linguistically significant units. For again there is no *other* way, given the same sound sequence, that A and B could independently arrive at identical interpretations. In theory it might be possible to hypothesize some non-linear system of analysis; but such a system would be far more complex for A and B to operate, apart from having less intuitive plausibility. Discrete segmentation of a linear continuum emerges as the simplest possible system for the operation of any fixed code using speech sounds as its sole channel of communication.

Orthodox linguistics thus has an internal elegance and harmony which do not become fully apparent until we see how the principles of arbitrariness and linearity are tacitly linked via the theory of telementation and the postulation of a fixed code. At first sight it might seem that arbitrariness and linearity have been selected merely because they are universal characteristics of speech. But if this were the reason other 'design features' (for example, productivity) would seem to have an equally strong claim. The rationale underlying Saussure's original choice might perhaps be stated most concisely as follows. If we define speech as oral communication, and communication as telementation, then the task of linguistics is to provide a theoretical framework for explaining what makes speech possible and how it may be systematically analysed. Given that we cannot discover any natural principles which explain how the forms of speech are determined by their meanings, then the simplest hypothesis would be that speaker and hearer share a fixed code of arbitrary signs, in which determinate meanings attach to determinate discrete segments in the flow of speech. Arbitrariness and linearity, therefore, are the two additional postulates which are necessary to put the linguist in a position to proceed immediately with the analysis of speech, once it is assumed that speech communication is a telementational process based on fixed codes. Arbitrariness and linearity are both crucial methodologically, because they constrain very rigorously the otherwise limitless possibilities for setting about the analysis of an unknown code.

'But what is wrong with this rationale?' it may well be asked. 'On what other theoretical basis could linguistics possibly proceed?' If linguistics is to be redefined, these are the two questions which must next be tackled.

LANGUAGES AS SYNCHRONIC SYSTEMS

What is wrong with a linguistics which defines itself in such a way as to set up a primary task of analysing postulated fixed codes whose only significant units are assumed to occur in linear sequences audibly manifested in the temporal flow of speech is that the enterprise is doomed in advance to fall foul of its own internal contradictions. Some of these had already occurred to Saussure, as is evident from the attempts he makes to deal with them. In spite of these attempts, and those of his successors, it remains difficult to avoid the conclusion that orthodox linguistics has failed to justify its own claim to be a science of speech communication. In assessing that claim both words in the phrase 'speech communication' are important. Orthodox linguistics did not claim to be a general science of speech *tout court* (which would have involved the anatomy and neurophysiology of the articulatory and auditory apparatus). Nor did it claim to be a general science of communication *tout court* (which would have involved the study of other signs than verbal signs). But it did claim to analyse speech in so far as speech was a form of communication, and communication in so far as communication was conducted by means of speech.

One general objection to a linguistics thus defined is that the fixed-code theory leads straight to what may be called the 'paradox of inquiry'. This arises in the following way. For any given word, either A and B share the same fixed code, in which case they will both assign the same meaning to that word; or else they will not assign the same meaning, in which case they do not share the same fixed code. Suppose, for example, the word is *quadrilateral*. A asks

'How many sides has a quadrilateral?' and B replies 'Four'. If A and B share the same fixed code, then A must already know the answer to the question; whereas in the alternative case A's question is one which it is impossible for B to understand correctly. It makes no difference in principle whether or not 'four' is the right answer, or how the word *quadrilateral* is defined. The point is that a fixed-code theory of speech communication must attribute exactly the same linguistic knowledge to A and B if communication is to be successful. On this theory, therefore, it is impossible for anyone to come to know the meaning of a word by asking another person. But this conclusion is paradoxical, since asking the meaning of a word is commonly held to be a normal and unproblematic function of speech communication; and furthermore this function is generally regarded as essential for the usual processes of language-learning.

A second objection is that if speech communication is indeed based on a fixed code shared by speakers and hearers it becomes extremely difficult to explain in any plausible way how the fixed code comes to be established in the first place. Every individual undergoes a unique apprenticeship to language, which is shared in full by no one else. Even within very restricted linguistic communities, such as the family, no two members are uniformly exposed to exactly the same learning experiences. The larger the community the less chance there is that any two individuals will have had the same opportunity to acquire exactly the same set of correlations between forms and meanings for purposes of communication. This, precisely, is one reason why it is sometimes argued that fixed codes could exist only at the idiolectal level. For languages are not like legal systems in which a central authority lays down rules and penalties to which all are subject, whether they like it or not. In other words, the fixed code with which A operates is presumably the unique product of A's individual linguistic experience, while the fixed code with which B operates is likewise the unique product of B's individual linguistic experience. But this conclusion contradicts the telementational account of speech communication itself; for we are left without the essential guarantee that A and B share one and the same fixed code. Saussure's *langue* is, very explicitly, an attempt to bridge the gap between individual and collectivity, and thus to resolve the apparent contradiction between the uniqueness of one's own linguistic psychohistory and the apparent facility with which one communicates with other members of the same linguistic community whom one has never previously met. But this attempt merely generates at one remove the no less intractable problem of accounting for how *la langue* comes into existence. Saussure turned his back on the question and simply denied that this was a problem linguists were required to deal with. But it is difficult to see how they can avoid it.

A third objection is that if the speech circuit depends on the operation of a fixed code then innovation becomes a theoretical impossibility. If A attempts to introduce a new word, B will certainly fail to understand it since *ex hypothesi* the word is not part of the code they share. On the other hand, if either A or B can introduce innovations which are communicationally successful, then the code is not fixed. This conflict between the demands of a fixed code and the possibility of linguistic change Saussure attempted to resolve by introducing a rigorous separation of synchronic from diachronic linguistics. However, this gives no explanation of how a transition from one synchronic system to its diachronic successor is possible for the language-users themselves. Thus the problem of innovation is dismissed, but not solved. The failure to deal with it has a particular irony, since the development of linguistics has been heavily dependent on the introduction of new terminology, and Saussure's *Cours* itself is a case in point. The work should have been incomprehensible if the theory of communication it advances is correct.

A fourth objection to a linguistics based on the fixed-code theory is that even if A and B *were* using the same fixed code they would never be able to be sure of this. For if B wishes to verify that the ideas A wished to convey are indeed those which B interprets A's utterance as conveying, B must either elicit further utterances from A or else assess A's reactions to further utterances by B, or both. The snag is that these tests will encounter verification problems of exactly the same order as raised by A's original utterance. Consequently the tests available to A and B to determine whether both are using the same linguistic system turn out to be either regressive or circular. This conclusion in itself does not automatically invalidate the fixed-code hypothesis; for nothing in that hypothesis entails that A and B realize, let alone could prove, that they share a common linguistic system. Nevertheless, there is something manifestly awkward about an explanation of any human social activity which leaves the participants theoretically unable to grasp what it is they are doing. For social activities are above all those in which the participants' intentions and interpretations of one another's behaviour are crucial factors in determining the course of the activity and the form which it takes.

A fifth objection is perhaps more powerful than any of these, at least as far as the academic status of linguistics is concerned. If linguistics deals with synchronic speech-systems (or *états de langue* in Saussurean terminology), and these systems are fixed codes, then they do not correspond to 'languages' in the everyday sense in which English, French, and German are reckoned to be the languages typically spoken by most people born and brought up in, say, the United Kingdom, France, and Germany. These are *not* fixed codes, whatever else they may be, because they are manifestly not uniform. Smith's English may not be the same as Brown's English. The French spoken by Dupont may differ from the French spoken by Duval. Such differences may affect not only pronunciation but grammar and vocabulary as well. Yet Smith is a native speaker of English, just as Brown is; and Dupont is a native speaker of French, just as Duval is. Thus it appears *prima facie* either that linguistics cannot deal with languages like English, French, and German; or if it does it cannot be dealing with fixed codes.

The orthodox strategy for dealing with this objection was again initiated by Saussure, who conceded that everyday language-names such as *English*, *French*, and *German* do not in practice correspond to those synchronic systems underlying speech communication which it is the business of linguistics to analyse. Instead, he claimed that each of these language-names designates a large and vaguely defined group of synchronic systems, historically related to one another. A more recent version of the same strategy is to claim that languages, in the sense in which English, French, and German are languages, are merely publicly constructed social artifacts; whereas the genuine object of linguistic analysis is the 'internalized grammar' of a competent speaker, which underlies those social artifacts.

Strategic manoeuvres of this kind parry the objection, but again do not solve the problem. For the question remains as to how descriptive linguists are to identify the existence of whatever system they are supposed to be describing. Saussure's own answer was that synchronic systems existed at the dialectal or subdialectal level: that is to say, although English as spoken in the year 1900 did not in its totality constitute a synchronic system, nevertheless 'British English' or – better still – 'educated Southern British English' in 1900 might well qualify. Later linguists saw even that restriction as itself problematic, and instead proposed that synchronic systems existed ultimately at the idiolectal level of the individual speaker.

This, however, is no solution either, since the descriptive linguist has no guarantee that the speech of any individual informant is always self-consistent. Smith's English may not be the same English on all occasions; it may depend on how Smith feels, who Smith is speaking to, what Smith wants, where Smith is, and a host of other factors. Worse still, if synchronic systems exist only at the idiolectal level, then *ex hypothesi* if Smith and Brown ever manage to engage in successful communication it will be sheer good luck. The identification of synchronic systems with idiolects is theoretically self-defeating for orthodox linguistics. It is no good for Smith to have a fixed code which is shared with no one else.

In short, the fixed-code theory lands linguistics in a dilemma. The business of the descriptive linguist is supposedly to analyse linguistic systems; but that task becomes impossible if the systems themselves cannot be reliably identified in use. The impossibility is on a par with that of describing the rules of various unknown games if the observer cannot be sure which game is being played on any given occasion. It has sometimes been suggested that the way out of this impasse is for the linguist as observer to describe the one language which does not present these difficulties of access, namely the linguist's own. But it then becomes unclear how linguists are supposed to check the internal consistency of their own linguistic practices or the accuracy of their own privileged observations.

The objections summarized above implicitly set certain goals for any proposed redefinition of linguistics. A redefined linguistics needs a theoretical basis which, as its minimal condition of viability, can be shown not to lead directly back into the theoretical morass of intractable orthodox problems.

IDEALIZATIONS IN LINGUISTICS

Although the objections mentioned so far already seem sufficient in themselves to call in question the validity of orthodox linguistics, nevertheless they are sometimes dismissed by defenders of the orthodox doctrine as irrelevant, on the ground that no one, from Saussure onwards, had ever seriously supposed that the conditions laid down in the fixed-code account of speech communication were those which normally obtain in real-life situations. The fixed code and the homogeneous speech community, it is claimed, are merely theoretical idealizations, which it is necessary for linguistics to adopt, just as other sciences adopt for theoretical purposes idealizations which do not correspond to the observable facts. Thus, for example, geometry postulates such idealizations as perfectly parallel lines and points with no dimensions; but these are not to be found in the world of visible, measurable objects. Nevertheless, it would be a mistake to protest on this ground that the theoretical foundations of geometry are inadequate or unsound. Analogously, it is held, idealizations of the kind represented by the fixed code are not only theoretically legitimate but theoretically essential in linguistics; and those who object to them simply fail to understand the role of idealization in scientific inquiry.

Unfortunately, this defence of the orthodox doctrine is based on a false comparison. Broadly speaking, two different types of intellectual idealization may be distinguished. In the exact sciences, and also in applied sciences such as architecture and economics, idealizations play an important role in processes of calculation. Any such idealization which was in practice discovered to be misleading or ineffectual when put to the test by being used as a basis for calculation would very soon be abandoned. In the humanities, by contrast, idealization plays an entirely different role. The ideal monarch, the ideal state, and the ideal mother are abstractions not set up in order to be used as a basis for calculation, but as prescriptive stereotypes on which to focus the discussion of controversial issues concerning how human beings should conduct themselves and how human affairs should be managed. But the ideal speech community, the ideal language, and the ideal speaker-hearer turn out to be neither one thing nor the other. They are neither abstractions to which items and processes in the real world may be regarded as approximating for purposes of calculation; nor are they models held up for purposes of exemplification or emulation. In fact they are, more mundanely, steps in a process of explanation; and as such subject to all the usual criticisms which explanatory moves may incur (including, for instance, that they fail to explain what they purport to explain).

What is particularly damning in the case of orthodox linguistics is that its idealized account of speech communication not merely fails to give a verifiable explanation of what passes for speech communication in the world of every day, but actually makes it theoretically impossible for a linguist proceeding on the basis of this idealization to come up with any linguistic analysis at all. Paradoxically, therefore, linguistics emerges as a 'science' in which the scientists have to ignore their own theoretical principles in order to be able to practice. Doubtless there are many disciplines in which, for practical purposes, theoretically illegitimate short cuts are taken every day. But there cannot be many which retain their status as sciences if the *only* way to proceed is for practitioners to flout established theory all the time.

SPEECH AND WRITING

If one were to rest content with making a merely negative, even if devastating, criticism of modern linguistics, there would be no need to proceed further. What has already been pointed out is the gross disparity – indeed contradiction – between the advertised aims of the descriptive linguist and the theoretical basis on which it is claimed these aims may be pursued. But there are other reasons, not so far mentioned, which call for a redefinition of linguistics.

First, a linguistics which confines the linguistic activities of speaker and hearer to the production and interpretation of arbitrary vocal signals articulated in a simple linear concatenation manifestly fails to deal with the reality of language in all its complexity. The segregationalist attempt to limit the analysis of language to its manifestations in speech is an attempt which fails because the limits it imposes are too narrow. But it is not merely that less stringent limits would be welcome. Rather, the primary theoretical issue to be faced is whether *any* a priori attempt to delimit language as a well demarcated field of inquiry can possibly be successful.

The reasons for rejecting the possibility of an a priori delimitation of language are overwhelming. Consider first the theoretical implications of the cultural fact that some societies have developed language in ways which are totally unknown in other societies. The most obvious historical example is the emergence of writing. Now if writing is possible, then so may be other potential forms of linguistic communication which now remain unexplored because they do not at present answer to human social needs or opportunities. But at some time in the future, possibly with the advent of new technologies, these potential forms of language may well come to be realized. We already know in advance, however, what the reaction of orthodox segregationalists will be. They will simply deny that any form of communication other than speech is language. For this has consistently been the position maintained by orthodox theorists throughout the present century. Bloomfield put it bluntly and unequivocally: 'Writing,' he asserted, 'is not language'. (Bloomfield 1935: 21) This is rather like denying that the piano is a musical instrument on the ground that its invention is comparatively recent and its use confined to a certain range of cultures. To deny the linguistic status of writing in turn invites an answer to the question of what writing actually is. Bloomfield's answer was equally dogmatic. For him, writing is 'merely a way of recording language' (Bloomfield 1935: 21). The trouble with this answer is that it is patently wrong. Language for Bloomfield is speech; and while it is true that writing may indeed be used to provide a record of speech, that is by no means its sole function, or even its major function. The notion that all written texts are records of words spoken prior to their inscription is manifestly absurd. Bloomfield was presumably as well aware of all this as anyone else. Why, then, did he refuse to accept it as relevant to the task of defining linguistics? The reason is not far to seek. Once it is theoretically conceded that language is not confined to oral expression but may also be expressed visually then the principle of linearity has to be abandoned as a foundational principle of linguistics. For visual signs are not necessarily linear.

Few critics have thoroughly examined the question of why Saussure selected linearity as his second principle of linguistics. The roots of the answer probably lie in Lessing's distinction between the spatial and the temporal arts, with which Saussure was no doubt familiar. According to Lessing:

> if it is true that painting and poetry in their imitations make use of entirely different means or symbols – the first, namely of form and colour in space, the second of articulated sounds in time – if these symbols indisputably require a suitable relation to the thing symbolized, then it is clear that the symbols arranged in juxtaposition can only express subjects of which the wholes or parts exist in juxtaposition; while

consecutive symbols can only express subjects of which the wholes or parts are consecutive.

(Lessing 1766: 91)

This passage presents a generalized theory of meaning as model of reality, well in advance of Wittgenstein.

Writing is a potentially awkward case for semiotic theories of this kind, because its external form belongs to the pictorial – i.e. visual – mode of expression, whereas its content is merely verbal. (At least, this appears to be the case from a European perspective. From an oriental point of view, the affinity between writing and painting is much closer.) The obvious way to accommodate writing, therefore, is to claim that in spite of its visual form it is merely a derivative representation of speech; and this is the classic segregationalist move.

Like Lessing, Saussure saw the basic theoretical issue as being how to distinguish language from pictorial art; and there is a case for saying that this has remained on the hidden agenda throughout the history of modern linguistics. Now to claim that the linguistic sign is arbitrary, even if that is true, is not enough. For pictorial representation in certain respects is also arbitrary. We do not begin to drive a wedge between the two until we insist on the fact that arbitrariness does not extend as far in both cases. 'Juxtaposition', to use Lessing's term, is arbitrary in speech, but not in painting. Whether the painter depicts one object to the left or to the right of another object is not an arbitrary matter; at least, not for European painting before Picasso. The left-right relationship is taken as signifying the actual disposition of the objects depicted. But if one word precedes or follows another word in speech, it cannot be taken as indicative of the spatial relationship of the objects designated by those words. It is in this sense that the principle of linearity is required to support the more general principle of arbitrariness. The two have to be taken together; and together they implicitly define language as a form of representation in which the sign is not merely arbitrary but linearly arbitrary; that is to say, spatio-temporally undetermined.

Now a redefinition of linguistics which abandons the principle of linearity no longer has any reason for insisting that speech is the sole or quintessential form of linguistic expression. Viewed in orthodox terms, the problem then becomes how to draw any

40

theoretical distinction between language and pictorial art. But it can be argued that linguistics can indeed be redefined in such a way as to sacrifice both the principle of linearity and the principle of arbitrariness, but nevertheless leave room for distinguishing linguistic representation from pictorial representation in so far as that distinction is relevant or necessary. This is the breakthrough on the hidden agenda of theoretical linguistics which orthodox theorists have so far declined to contemplate.

There are in any case independent reasons for recognizing that although there are linguistic connections between speech and writing, writing cannot be considered merely a functional extension of speech. One reason is simply that it is possible to learn to write a language without knowing how to speak it. Another is that there are written languages used for communication by people unable to understand one another's speech, even though the same written language can be used to transcribe both. A third reason has to do with the psycholinguistics of reading. According to the orthodox segregationalist view, the essential difference between reading the words 'Open the door' and hearing the words 'Open the door' is that the reader has learnt a set of audiographic correlations which make it possible to reconstruct from a series of alphabetic characters the abstract phonetic image of the spoken words. In short, written communication between A and B is exactly the same as spoken communication except that in addition to the triggering of concepts by phonetic images and vice versa there is an extra process by which phonetic images trigger corresponding configurations of visible marks and vice versa. This, allegedly, explains why A and B can dispense with vocalization in written communication, but nevertheless transmit exactly the same message as would have been transmitted by speech. However, there is nowadays general agreement among psychologists who have made a special study of reading, and in particular of various forms of dyslexia, that this theory, which in effect postulates that we read and write by matching sounds to graphic symbols and vice versa, is far too simplistic to account for the complex cognitive processes associated with literacy. Yet this is the only theory which strictly squares with the segregationalist account of speech and its relationship to writing. In other words, it attributes to A and B a second fixed code of audiographic correlations, which is based on and supplements their primary fixed code of correlations between sounds and concepts. Anything less simplistic automatically raises problems for the segregationalist thesis that writing has no linguistic status of its own.

VERBAL AND NON-VERBAL SIGNS

The controversy surrounding the relationship between speech and writing has a long history (Harris 1986). The point which deserves emphasis here is that the case of literacy is only one example – although a particularly clear and well documented example – of the more general problem of discerning where in human affairs language begins and ends. For this is coterminous with the problem of defining linguistics itself.

That problem would be no less intractable if writing had never been invented; for it arises no less acutely in the case of pre-literate societies than in the case of societies which have developed forms of writing. In neither case is any solution afforded by the arbitrary decision to restrict linguistics to the study of speech phenomena. For the problem then becomes how to segregate speech phenomena from their embedding in a continuum of communication. Speech, clearly, cannot be simply equated with phonation. Many of the sounds which register on a spectrograph or an oscilloscope do not belong to 'speech' in the sense in which that term has been appropriated by orthodox linguistics. On the other hand, much of what orthodox linguistics dismisses as non-verbal is highly pertinent to the interpretation of the sounds speakers make when they engage in speech communication.

The problem was long ago recognized as one pertinent to linguistic theory; for example, by J. R. Firth. Did not Firth, in the wake of Malinowski, recognize the limitations of a segregationalist approach to language when he wrote of the 'interlocking' of speech and non-speech? Witness, for instance, the following quotation:

> The meaning of any particular instance of everyday speech is intimately interlocked not only with an environment of particular sights and sounds, but deeply embedded in the living processes of persons maintaining themselves in society.
>
> (Firth 1952: 13)

In these words, there appears to be a clear recognition that speech cannot be divorced from its integration into a non-verbal context. Nevertheless, recognizing a truth is not to be equated with realizing its theoretical implications. Firthian linguistics never fully realized those implications, in spite of the great emphasis it laid on the importance of contextual factors. Firth himself, as a recently published critique of his work shows (Love 1988), although rejecting Saussure's *langue*, pioneered a form of linguistic analysis which in practice compromises with Saussurean orthodoxy all along the line. In short, Firthian methodology is inconsistent with Firth's proclaimed principles.

What Firth, in common with other critics of the segregationalist approach, in the end shied away from was the prospect of redefining linguistics in such a way as to take account of a simple fact of everyday experience. In linguistic communication, what people do *not* say is just as important as what they *do* say. If A utters the words 'Open the door' and B in response says nothing but simply opens it, then B has exhibited a knowledge of English which *pro tanto* not only matches A's but is no less clearly demonstrated than in A's utterance. This is not to say that opening the door is the only way in which B might demonstrate a linguistic proficiency adequate to this particular communication situation; nor that it is the ultimate criterion of B's relevant linguistic knowledge. Both these assumptions would lead to a linguistics defined on a narrowly behaviouristic basis.

Nevertheless, B's behaviour in this situation *is* communicationally relevant, and here the theoretical baby must not be thrown out with the behaviouristic bathwater. For there is no reason to deny that B's opening the door is a *linguistic* act, just as much as A's utterance. That is to say, opening the door *in this particular situation* is a response which qualifies as 'linguistic' no less indubitably than A's vocalization. It is not to say that every time a door is opened linguistic communication is taking place; any more than it is to say that every time a given sequence of sounds is produced linguistic communication is taking place. But to acknowledge that in opening the door B makes a linguistically appropriate contextual response to A's utterance is to recognize that B's actions also are signs, on an equal footing with the signs expressed vocally by A. By so acting, B in turn signals to A; and, specifically, signals an interpretation of A's own utterance. It is this reciprocity which is constitutive of communication. By focusing exclusively on A's utterance, orthodox linguistics introduces an asymmetry which simply ignores the mutual dependency of A's and B's communicative acts.

The theoretical implications of this mutual dependency are far-reaching. Both A's verbal act and B's non-verbal act have to be seen as integrated constituents in an interactive continuum of communication. Divorced from that continuum, neither has any communicational significance whatsoever. Any attempt to give a systematic analysis of what A does independently of what B does rests on a misconception of what is going on. It is like trying to describe a game of tennis as if it were being played by only one person, and the player on the other side of the net did not exist. Such a description, we may be sure, however exhaustively it appears to cover the actions of the single player selected for attention, cannot make any sense of the game being played.

There are various corollaries for the linguist which follow from this. Some will be dealt with in the remainder of this paper. But before proceeding to those the first essential is to realize how radical a redefinition of linguistics is called for simply in order to accommodate the integration of spoken and unspoken signs in this very elementary type of case.

Orthodox linguistics has no way of dealing with the relationship between A's utterance and B's actions because it cannot deal with the description of non-vocal signalling. Even if it waived the requirement of vocalization, it cannot analyse what B does in terms of the segmentation of a linear sequence into units which match the three verbal signs A uttered. If it could, then there would be no hindrance to arguing that a systematic description based on the principles of arbitrariness and linearity could be extended to cover the integration of A's utterance and B's non-verbal response. But this would only work if the structure of linguistic communication were much simpler than in fact it is. It might work, for instance, if languages were signalling systems no more complex than highway traffic lights; or if A and B were the builder and his assistant described in the opening paragraphs of Wittgenstein's *Philosophical Investigations* (Wittgenstein 1953). The trouble is that speech is underpinned by non-verbal communication which is vastly more complex than these simple cases exemplify.

If an integrational linguistics starts from the premiss that not all linguistic signs are vocal signs, then immediately it must reject most of what has passed for linguistic analysis in western universities for the past fifty years. For those forms of analysis were predicated precisely upon the assumption which an integrational approach must disavow; namely, that the systematicity of speech is self-contained and can be described without reference to what lies outside the speech circuit. There can be no question of retrospectively accepting work based on that assumption as having provided a preliminary ground-clearing operation, on which it is now possible to proceed to construct fully integrated analyses. An integrational linguistics cannot be built on segregationalist foundations. To cherish that hope would be to make all over again exactly the same mistake as has already been made in the history of the subject. Tinkering with the orthodox paradigm must not be confused with redefining linguistics.

AN INTEGRATIONALIST PROGRAMME

By rejecting a telementational model of communication and substituting an integrationalist model (i.e. one in which the sign is not given in advance of the communication situation but is itself constituted in the context of that situation by virtue of the integrational role it fulfils) the foundation is laid for an entirely new approach to the study of language. It becomes possible to treat linguistic communication as a continuum of interaction which may be manifested both verbally and non-verbally. This requires a theoretical basis which is quite different from the theoretical basis of orthodox linguistics. But exactly how?

An integrationalist redefinition of linguistics can dispense with at least the following theoretical assumptions: (i) that the linguistic sign is arbitrary; (ii) that the linguistic sign is linear; (iii) that words have meanings; (iv) that grammar has rules; and (v) that there are languages. This last point, despite its paradoxical appearance, follows from the first four. In effect, to dispense with the first four assumptions is, precisely, to say that linguistics does not need to postulate the existence of languages as part of its theoretical apparatus. What is called in question, in other words, is whether the concept of 'a language', as defined by orthodox modern linguistics, corresponds to any determinate or determinable object of analysis at all, whether social or individual, whether institutional or psychological. If there is no such object, it is difficult to evade the conclusion that modern linguistics has been based upon a myth.

A demythologized linguistics (that is to say, a linguistics liberated from the telementational fallacy) would sponsor a type of programme which will be briefly outlined in what follows. Once a telementational model is rejected, one can reject along with it the orthodox constraints on what a language is conceived to be. These constraints flow from the fact that the telementational model requires the assumption of a predetermined plan or fixed code which ensures in advance that the hearer, if all goes well, will be able to receive exactly the message that the speaker intended to convey. It would not do to have a system under which the utterance conveying A's message is interpreted by B as conveying some different message. Such a system could not be a language, according to the telementational theory, because it would fail to ensure communication between A and B.

This being so, the telementational model automatically imposes what may be called an 'invariance condition' on the language. Whatever may vary as between one speaker and another, or between the conveyance of a given message on one occasion and the conveyance of the same message on another occasion, cannot count as part of the language. This is why a segregationalist linguistics, although restricting linguistic communication to speech, cannot deal with all the information for which speech acts as a vehicle. It must exclude, for example, what the speech signal may convey concerning the speaker's sex, emotional state and personal identity. This is because, in order to ensure the possibility of communication throughout the community, the linguistic 'code book' which any member of the community uses for sending and receiving messages must be exactly the same as that used by every other member, at least in theory. To the extent that in practice the invariance condition is not fulfilled, communication between members will be at best partial or faulty.

It follows from this that the telementational model requires the ideal community to have a language in which all the basic units are determinate and all the rules which govern their combinations and interpretations are determinate. For otherwise there is no possibility of a common code book for the whole community. This stipulation is central to the orthodox language myth concerning synchronic systems. It does not in itself resolve the problem of deciding how much of the communicational process is accounted for by knowledge of the language. But what it does settle in advance is that the expressions of a language have to be determinate both in respect of 'form' and in respect of 'meaning'. There must be fixed rules for deciding whether a given sequence of sounds does or does not represent an expression of the language and, if it does, for identifying that expression; and there must also be fixed rules for assigning the right interpretation to any expression thus identified.

In this way, before any decision has been made about what in principle is to count as 'form' or as 'meaning', the communication model already imposes a bi-planar structuring on the language system, in the sense that no expression with a determinate meaning can fail to have a determinate form corresponding to that meaning, and no expression with a determinate form can fail to have a corresponding determinate meaning. Although for orthodox descriptive purposes the two planes of form and meaning may be considered independently, it is the network of specific correlations between them which makes communication possible. It would be of no avail for the language-user to know all the forms of the language, and all the meanings as well, but not to know which forms had which meanings.

It was Saussure who first carried through this consequence of adopting a telementational model to its logical conclusion by actually defining the linguistic sign in terms of the psychological association between form and meaning. In orthodox linguistics, not only the individual sign but the whole structure of grammar is likewise tacitly envisaged in terms of telementation. 'The function of a grammar,' we are told, 'is to link meaning with sound' (Bartsch and Vennemann 1973: 3). In other words, grammatical rules are devices for ensuring a consistent correspondence between the form of an utterance and the ideas it conveys. Saussure's distinction between synchronic and diachronic is above all required in his theory in order to provide the logical space within which a telementational model may operate.

In order to redefine linguistics successfully it is essential to reject the whole mythology of language structure which derives from a telementational model of communication. An integrationalist redefinition is in a position to do this because it adopts a perspective which, in Saussurean terms, is neither synchronic nor diachronic but panchronic. It considers as pertinent to linguistic communication both the integration of simultaneously occurring events and also the integration of present events with past events and anticipated future events. This integration is governed by a single 'principle of cotemporality', which postulates a chronological parity between linguistic and non-linguistic events in human experience.

This principle, which orthodox linguistics fails to recognize, is of basic importance if we wish to have a theory of language which can explain how and why communication invariably proceeds on the assumption that every linguistic act is integrated into the individual's experience as a unique event, which has never before occurred and will never recur. Without this principle the theorist cannot even begin to explain the basic and universal metalinguistic concept of 'repetition'. To repeat what was said is perhaps the most general and primitive mechanism involved in the transmission of linguistic information in all societies of which we have any record. It is the mechanism on which the function of the messenger depends in every pre-literate culture.

The orthodox 'principle of linearity' derives what validity it possesses from being a special case of the more general principle of cotemporality. Once we recognize the latter we can dispense with the former. Furthermore, this replacement enables us to give theoretical recognition to linguistic signs which are non-linear in structure, even though their use is governed by the principle of cotemporality.

The orthodox 'principle of arbitrariness' is, from an integrationalist point of view, simply an irrelevance. It makes no difference whether a given sign is arbitrary (in the orthodox sense) or not; for its significance is always a function of its integration into a particular communication situation. To insist on arbitrariness as a defining feature of the linguistic sign is a futile attempt to draw the boundary between the linguistic and the non-linguistic at a point where it cannot be drawn. This, in turn, is the result of treating the linguistic sign as a decontextualized unit, having a form and a meaning whose relationship can be considered in isolation from the actual employment of the sign in any given situation.

But this is not all. From an integrationalist point of view it might be said that the principle of arbitrariness is doubly irrelevant. For it presupposes that each sign has a meaning; whereas this is an assumption which the integrationalist neither needs nor endorses. By denying that words, or other signs, have meanings what the integrationalist is rejecting is the orthodox claim that there is some invariant semantic value which attaches to a linguistic sign in all circumstances, and from which its interpretation is derived by those who use it. This is the myth of meaning institutionalized in dictionaries, and it is logically required by the telementational account of how speech communication works. For purposes of an integrational analysis, however, the concept of meaning may be dispensed with and replaced by that of communicational function. The crucial difference is that the communicational function of a sign is always contextually determined and derives from the network of integrational relations which obtain in a particular situation.

Likewise, from an integrational point of view, grammar is contextually determined and therefore cannot be stated in terms of decontextualized rules. Since the notion of a rule which varies from one occasion to another is a notion which lacks coherence, it follows that for an integrationalist grammar has no rules. Nor is the province of grammar limited to the narrow domain it occupies in orthodox linguistics. Thus, for instance, if A asks a question and B gives a non-verbal response, there is for the integrationalist a grammatical relation between the question and the non-verbal response, just as there would be for the orthodox linguist between a question and a verbal answer. In other words, the domain of grammar is the whole domain of combinatorial relationships which are contextually relevant to establishing communicational sense. A raised eyebrow may be as relevant to what is said as the intonation contour of a sentence, or the length of the pause between one sentence and the next.

Finally, it follows that integrationalism has no theoretical place for the concept of a language in the narrow sense recognized by orthodox linguistics, where languages are construed, precisely, as sets of decontextualized rules, not only grammatical, but phonological and semantic rules as well. On the other hand, the integrationalist recognizes the lay metalinguistic distinctions that are drawn between one language and another, for such distinctions are among those in terms of which lay members of a linguistic community construe their own linguistic experience. For it is not that lay people are mistaken or misguided when they classify some words as 'English', others as 'French', others as 'German', and so on. What is mistaken is the way in which orthodox linguistics has treated an explicandum as a theoretical postulate. Starting from the postulate that linguistics deals in the first instance with determinate rule-based systems called 'languages' has the effect of standing the problem on its head. That makes it almost impossible to arrive at any clear understanding of how such concepts arise and

ROY HARRIS

what role they play in our conceptualization of the communicational space in which human beings live. Languages are functions
of communicational processes, not vice versa.

What, then, is the integrationalist programme for linguistics?
Integrationalism redefines linguistics as a mode of inquiry into the
construction and articulation of our linguistic experience. It
inquires not into the hypothetical structure of abstract linguistic
systems, nor into their even more hypothetical representations in
the human brain, but into the everyday integrational mechanisms
by means of which the reality of the linguistic sign as a fact of life is
established. For this purpose, in contradistinction to all previous
linguistic programmes, it rejects any a priori attempt to cir-
cumscribe the phenomena of language or to draw a distinction
between language and non-language which will be valid in each
and every case. Instead, it delimits its own sphere of investigation
by reference to dimensions of communicational relevance which
apply to all forms of sign behaviour in human communities. Such
an inquiry may conveniently distinguish between three different
scales or levels of relevance, depending on the mode of our
involvement in communicational processes. One scale, which may
be termed 'macrosocial', deals with factors which situate any given
communication in its particular historical and cultural context. A
second, which we may term 'biomechanical', deals with factors of a
physiological and physical nature which determine the parameters
of communication within that situation. The third scale is the
integrational scale itself, concerned with communication as a
function of the individual's experience in the context of a given
situation.

Any episode of communication, in its totality, will call for
analysis on all three scales. To the macrosocial scale belong factors
of the kind which orthodox linguistics relegates to such subdis-
ciplines as dialectology and sociolinguistics. To the biomechanical
scale belong factors of the kind dealt with in articulatory, auditory,
and acoustic phonetics, along with others which relate to sight and
other sensory capacities. To the integrational scale belong factors
relating to the psychohistories of the individual participants, which
affect how they negotiate and make sense of the episode in
question. The episode itself is the unique integrational product of
all these factors.

Accordingly, an integrational linguistics will focus on typically
different questions from those which have preoccupied and still

50

preoccupy the orthodox linguist. Investigations which are at most of marginal interest within the framework of linguistic orthodoxy become central. Whereas the attempt to give a mathematically precise formulation to rules of grammar can tell us nothing about how most people construct and articulate their own linguistic experience, we may on the contrary learn a great deal about this by asking what everyday metalinguistic vocabulary they use. Grammatical formalizations reveal more about the grammarian than about the language which the grammarian claims to be formalizing. Even the pursuit of abstract linguistic universals will teach us less about the human mind than studying how, in specific situations, human beings combine verbal and non-verbal signalling for purposes of communication, and how they apportion the communicational load between verbal and non-verbal devices. The number of parts of speech a language has (however a linguist decides to count them) cannot be more important than distinguishing the different integrational functions that different types of word fulfil in discourse. In short, the strategies and assumptions people bring to bear on the communicational tasks of daily activity, tasks they are obliged to deal with by whatever means they can, are all an integrational linguistics needs to study in order to advance our understanding of what language is and the part it plays in our lives.

An integrational approach thus makes possible a thoroughgoing demythologization of linguistics. The first step in the demythologizing process is simply to convince linguists that no disastrous consequences ensue from abandoning the hallowed assumptions of orthodox linguistic theory. The case is roughly parallel to the demythologization of economics which was accomplished earlier this century by theorists led by John Maynard Keynes. The prevailing economic myth which the Keynesians attacked was, as it happens, one which bears striking similarities to the currently prevalent myth of orthodox linguistics. These similarities are not merely coincidental, but to trace the historical interconnections falls outside the scope of the present paper. They are similarities which hinge on a common concept of 'value'. Just as orthodox linguistics treats sounds as having meanings by standing for concepts or for objects and persons in the external world, so the basic idea of economic theory which the Keynesians called in question was the idea that a pound note had a value by standing for a quantity of gold. Confidence in the so-called 'gold standard' went hand in hand with the popular view that pound notes in themselves were worthless because they were 'only pieces of paper'. The linguistic parallel here is the view that speech itself is meaningless because spoken words are just vocal noises. It was widely feared that if the Keynesian view prevailed and the so-called 'gold standard' was abandoned, then the honest savings of millions of poor working people would automatically become valueless. So the first task in the Keynesian demythologization of economics was to argue that nothing disastrous would follow from coming off the 'gold standard', because the so-called 'gold standard' was itself part of a myth about finance.

One naïve reaction to arguments against the telementational model is to ask what alternative explanation can be proposed of how it is possible for human beings to convey their ideas to one another. But those who demand this alternative account merely demonstrate how completely bemused they are by the language myth in question. It is rather like asking a Keynesian what alternative standard should replace the 'gold standard': perhaps a 'silver standard', or a 'copper standard'? The point of the term *demythologization* here is that there is no question of an alternative account. Myths do not have alternatives. To ask for an alternative is a sign of having failed to recognize the myth as a myth.

There is one last point worth making in connection with demythologization. Myths cannot be shown to be false, because myths are never founded on propositions which were demonstrable in the first place. Keynesian economics did not demonstrate that 'gold standard' economics was wrong, but merely that faith in the 'gold standard' was unnecessary, unhelpful, and in various ways obfuscating and harmful. The Keynesian strategy is to point out that the assumption that currency notes are pieces of paper standing for quantities of precious metals fails to make sense of economic reality, where in practice money functions as a complex of mechanisms which facilitate the distribution of goods and services. Money does not in addition need to 'stand for' anything. Analogously in the linguistic case, once we see that language can be treated as a complex of mechanisms for facilitating communication there is no need to insist that linguistic signs 'stand for' anything else in addition. Nor need anyone fear that a linguistics which abandons the writing of grammars and dictionaries has abandoned linguistic inquiry altogether. On the contrary, it is only when linguistics has advanced beyond the grammar and the dictionary that the serious business of linguistic inquiry will have begun.

3

THE LOCUS OF LANGUAGES IN A REDEFINED LINGUISTICS*

Nigel Love

I

Linguistic theory is dominated by two interlocking ideas. The first idea is that communication by means of language is a matter of thought-transference, and it was first articulated, as far as twentieth-century linguistics is concerned, by Saussure. Linguistic communication is envisaged by Saussure as follows. In the brain of a given individual, 'facts of consciousness which we shall call concepts are associated with representations of linguistic signs or acoustic images by means of which they are expressed'[1] (Saussure 1922: 28). If A wishes to communicate with B, he utters representations of the acoustic images corresponding to the concepts he wants to express. B recognizes the acoustic images of which A has uttered representations, and matches them with the corresponding concepts in his own brain. Thus A is able to impart his ideas because he knows which acoustic images correspond to those ideas in the *langue* which A and B share, while B is able to understand A because he knows which ideas correspond to the acoustic images of which he hears representations.

This thesis is less than obviously acceptable as a theoretical postulate for a science of language. In the first place, in so far as it might qualify as a candidate-explanation of communication at all, it purports to explain only successful communication. But the criteria for communicational success are mysterious. The Saussurean theory of communication offers to explain what it is that has happened when a hearer has fully or properly understood a speaker, but the usefulness of such an account depends on there

* I am grateful to the following for comments on the arguments presented here: Rudolf Botha, Lily Knezevich, Roger Lass, Trevor Pateman, Talbot Taylor.

being some generally accepted prior notion of what constitutes full or proper understanding, and some objective way of telling when it has been achieved. Secondly, before it could serve as the basis for a serious analysis of what happens when we speak to one another, the transference metaphor would require explication. Waves of varying air pressure resulting from activity in the speaker's vocal tract impinge on the hearer's eardrums. But there is no literal sense in which these sound waves 'convey' or 'transport' anything.

The idea that there is a state of affairs, recurrently arising in the course of linguistic interaction, which is uncontroversially identifiable as 'full' or 'proper' understanding of what was said, is based on a distortedly simple concept of 'understanding' itself.[2] For instance, one writer opens his account of how the study of generative grammar can improve our grasp of the psychobiological basis for language by stating baldly that '[children] come to be able to speak and understand speech effortlessly, instantaneously and subconsciously' (Lightfoot 1982: x). Now, if taken literally, this doctrine is obviously false, at least as far as understanding speech is concerned. It does not take much reflection on one's linguistic experience for a welter of possible obstacles to understanding to come to mind. One's interlocutor may have a speech impediment or a foreign accent. The telephone line may be faulty, or there may be clashing cymbals next door. One's command of the language being spoken may be non-native or non-existent. Points of this sort are so obvious that the claim about effortless and instantaneous understanding must surely involve a large idealization. But just what is the idealization in play here? Suppose we eliminate, for theoretical purposes, the diverse and randomly chosen obstructive phenomena just listed. The ideal would then be a case where there are no external environmental hindrances to the effectiveness of the communicational channel, and where speaker and hearer are both physically normal and speak the same dialect of the same language. Perhaps this is a reasonable idealization: if such circumstances obtain, we might say, it is unobjectionable to speak of effortless, instantaneous understanding. But what does such 'understanding' involve? For suppose we now add to the list of hypothetical impediments to understanding the possibility that the hearer may lack adequate acquaintance with the subject under discussion. Would it be reasonable to extend the idealization to cover such cases – to stipulate, that is, that for purposes of the idealization speaker and hearer should be deemed to have equal knowledge of (and, for that matter, interest in) what is being said? If so, then the Lightfootian doctrine of effortless, instantaneous understanding fails to apply to all those numerous communicational exchanges where, roughly speaking, the speaker tells the hearer something he does not already know. The classroom, for instance, is a place where understanding is often notoriously far from effortless or instantaneous. And classrooms, or their equivalents, are important venues for language-use in a great many societies. A linguistic theory which started by idealizing them away would not have much to be said for it. One imagines, on the contrary, that we are supposed to invoke here a distinction between understanding the 'language-as-such' and understanding what the language may be used to say. But the problem with that is that the language-as-such turns out on investigation to be hard to pin down.

One point which Lightfootians fail to take into account is that being a native speaker of a language by no means guarantees the ability to understand utterances in it. Consider the following extract from a newspaper column:

> When dummy went down, I realised that 6S would make if suits broke well and the diamond honours were favourably placed. I therefore decided to assume that twelve tricks were not readily available, hoping thereby to beat all the pairs going down in slam contracts and to make more tricks than those who had lingered in game. I won the opening heart lead in dummy, drew trumps in two rounds and cashed the ace of clubs. I then ruffed a heart in the closed hand, paving the way for an elimination, and cashed the king of clubs, discarding a diamond from dummy. When the ten of clubs appeared from East, I did not need to look any further for twelve tricks: I ran the jack of clubs, throwing another diamond from dummy, and subsequently discarded a third diamond on the established nine of clubs. I was then able to ruff two diamonds in dummy, thereby collecting twelve tricks by way of five spade tricks and two ruffs, one heart, one diamond and three clubs.
>
> (Markus 1982)

One imagines that many speakers of English will not make much of this. But the linguist would be hard pressed to argue that this is because it is not English. It is clearly English, and yet speakers of English may have difficulty in understanding it. What is the source of the difficulty? It is not, for the most part, the obscurity of the vocabulary. Apart from *ruff, dummy, slam contract,* and a few others, not many of the words in the passage are in themselves obscure to anyone with at least a slight acquaintance with the practice of card-playing. And, apart from the occasional oddity (*when dummy went down, those who had lingered in game,* where common nouns are used without an article, as though they were proper names), the syntax is quite straightforward too. Nor does the problem arise from the fact that the words are used metaphorically or in some other non-literal way: what we have here is a perfectly sober and prosaically literal account of a game of bridge. The conclusion must be that those who find it incomprehensible do so because of their lack of familiarity, not with the English language, but with bridge.

Lack of the relevant extralinguistic knowledge may hinder understanding of the linguistic expressions used to describe that piece of the world. But the Lightfootian position must presumably be that although we understand the *language* of the passage (because we are native speakers of the language of which it is a sample), where we fall down is in our grasp of the situation being described. But this seems to be a distinction without a difference.

This point is confirmed if we examine a typical illustrative account of the distinction (Leech 1974: 7–8). *My uncle always sleeps standing on one toe* is said to be factually, rather than linguistically (or contingently, rather than necessarily) absurd. It just happens to be the case that human beings cannot sleep in that posture. But if the world had been ordered differently they might have been able to, and if they were, there would be nothing absurd about such a sentence. Whereas no conceivable reordering of the world could eliminate the absurdity of a sentence like *my uncle always sleeps awake,* for if my uncle is asleep then, by definition, he is not awake, and if he is awake, then he is not asleep. But there is no very obvious reason why these explanations of the two kinds of absurdity should not be transposed. Instead of saying that it is the nature of standing on one toe that makes talk of sleeping in that position absurd, why should we not locate the absurdity in the conjunction of the meanings of the expressions *sleeps* and *standing on one toe*? Conversely, it might be argued that what makes sleeping awake inconceivable is not the incompatibility of the meanings of

sleep and *awake*, but the incompatibility of the states of consciousness referred to by those words. Our understanding of sleep and
wakefulness is such that we have no (non-absurd) use for sentences
about creatures sleeping awake. But it might have been the case
that there were animals which exhibit a state of consciousness that
bears some of the characteristics of both. If so, talk of them
sleeping awake might make perfectly good sense. The non-
existence of such creatures, if it is a fact, is as much a fact about
'the world' as is the non-existence of uncles who sleep standing on
one toe.

Why does linguistic theory require the postulation of languages-
as-such, and of semantic knowledge of them as something strictly
distinct from knowledge of the extralinguistic world? The answer
brings us to the second idea which has dominated modern
linguistic theory. This is the idea that languages are devices
designed to permit the thought-transference which constitutes
linguistic communication. They do so by providing a context-
neutral system of correspondences between forms and meanings. In
Saussure's terms, a language (*langue*) is a set of signs uniting
concepts (meanings) and acoustic images (forms). A language is a
fixed code of correlations between forms and meanings, and it is
the shared access of interlocutors to that code that makes
communication possible.

As may readily be seen, these two ideas form a closed circle. The
fixed-code concept of a language is required to explain how
linguistic communication is possible, while a particular view of
what communication is vindicates that concept of a language. If
language-use is the swapping of messages in a language-as-such,
then there must be a language-as-such with which to do it. On the
other hand, the idea that there are such things as context-neutral
languages-as-such is underwritten by the thought-transference
theory of communication. The trouble is that linguistic communication is not a matter of transferring thoughts from one mind
to another, while the analysis of languages as devices which enable
thought-transference to take place is fraught with difficulties.

Another way of demonstrating the mysterious elusiveness of
languages-as-such is to consider some of these difficulties. Concentrating on just one aspect of the problem of vindicating the idea
of languages as fixed sets of form-meaning correspondences, let us
consider the question of how to identify the pleremes[3] of a
language: that is, the minimal units of meaningful linguistic form.

It should be said at the outset that some theorists scarcely recognize a problem here at all. Thus Firth (1935: 25ff.) offers a phonological, grammatical, and semantic analysis of an English form transcribable as [bɔːd], as abstracted from such potential utterances as [wɪtʃbɔːd], [bɔːdəvstʌdɪz], [bɔːdiː], [bɔːdtədɛθ], without explaining what it is that makes [bɔːd] in these sequences a 'form', as opposed to (on the one hand) such sequences as [tʃbɔː] or [bɔːdəv] or (on the other) [bɔːd] in [səbɔːdɪnət] or [hiːbɔːdɑʊnɑnɪt]. He simply assumes that utterances can be analysed terances can be analysed into 'elements and components'. So *circumvent*, for example, is an English 'primitive' or word-base, while *fishy* or *restless* are 'derivatives'. 'It follows from this', says Firth, 'that we recognise such categories as word-base, stem, affix and other formatives, and eventually what we call sounds' (Firth 1935: 20). On the contrary, our capacity to analyse utterances into their constituent stems, affixes, etc. (that is, into their constituent pleremes) is by no means uncontroversially established, as emerges from consideration of other theorists' attempts to outline systematic procedures for doing so. By way of example,[4] let us consider Bloomfield.

The Bloomfieldian plereme is called the 'morpheme'. In analysing utterances into morphemes, according to Bloomfield, we must first note that linguistic forms may be either simple or complex. Complex forms are those which are to be treated as consisting of a number of simple forms. For example, *John ran* is an English complex form consisting of the simple forms *John* and *ran*. The reason for saying so is that if *John ran* is compared with *John fell*, 'we recognise at once that these two forms, *John ran* and *John fell*, are in part phonetically alike, since both of them contain an element *John* [dʒɔn], and our practical knowledge tells us that the meanings show a corresponding resemblance: whenever a form contains the phonetic element [dʒɔn] the meaning involves a certain man or boy in the community' (Bloomfield 1935: 159). That is, if when comparing utterances we recognize recurrent likenesses of form associated with the same meaning, then we are dealing with a complex form which stands in need of further analysis into its constituent simple forms. A simple form is one which 'bears no partial phonetic-semantic resemblance to any other form' (Bloomfield 1935: 161).

Simple linguistic forms may be either 'free' or 'bound'. *John* is a free form because it can occur not only in combination with other forms as part of a complex form, but also in isolation (as in the utterance 'John!'). The -*y* of *Johnny*, on the other hand, is a bound form, as it never occurs alone. 'In the same way, familiar with the forms *play* and *dance*, we may hear the forms *playing* and *dancing*, and then hope in vain to hear an isolated -*ing* . . .[5] In spite of the fact that some components do not occur alone, but only as parts of larger forms, we nevertheless call these components linguistic forms, since they are phonetic forms, such as [i] or [iŋ], with constant meanings' (Bloomfield 1933: 159–60).

Although not free to occur alone, a form like -*y*, as in *Johnny*, nonetheless occurs more widely than as part of this one complex form. The same -*y* appears in, for instance, *Billy* and *Danny*. But other bound forms are denied even this limited freedom of occurrence. The *cran*- of *cranberry*, for instance, never figures except as the first part of this one word *cranberry*.[6] 'However, since it has a constant phonetic form, and since its meaning is constant, in so far as a *cranberry* is a definite kind of *berry*, different from all other kinds, we say that *cran*-, too, is a linguistic form. Experience shows that we do well to generalize this instance: *unique elements* which occur only in a single combination, are linguistic forms' (Bloomfield 1935: 160).

Single linguistic forms, defined in this way, are 'morphemes'. Most utterances, however, are instances of complex forms. A complex form, says Bloomfield, 'is entirely made up, so far as its phonetically definable constituents are concerned, of morphemes' (Bloomfield 1935: 161). A morpheme is a single form with a constant meaning. But the meaning of a complex form, consisting of more than one morpheme, cannot be treated simply as the adjunction of the constant meanings of its constituent morphemes. Therefore the analysis of complex forms involves more than stating their morphemic composition. For example, *Bill hit John* and *John hit Bill* differ in meaning, not in virtue of any differences in the meanings of the constituent morphemes, but because of 'the two different orders in which the morphemes are uttered' (Bloomfield 1935: 163).

Ordering is one of four factors identified by Bloomfield as involved in arranging the simple forms of a language meaningfully. The others are 'modulation', 'phonetic modification', and 'selection'. Significant for the discussion at this point is phonetic modification.

Phonetic modification is 'a change in the primary phonemes of a form' (Bloomfield 1935: 163). The form *do* is ordinarily (in

Bloomfield's transcription) [duw] and *not* [nɔt]. But, when they are combined, [duw] may become [dow] and [nɔt] [nt], giving the form *don't*. This is an example of optional modification, in that the unmodified combination [duwnɔt] may also occur. An example of compulsory modification would be the change of [djuwk] to [dʌtʃ] when the form *duke* finds itself in combination with the form *-ess* (*duchess*). Another example, different in that one cannot so readily talk of modification of a basic 'unmodified' form, is the occurrence of the three alternants [ɪz], [z], [s] that occur in plural nouns (*glasses* [glɑsɪz], *pens* [pɛnz], *books* [bʊks]).

[ɪz], [z], [s] exemplify what Bloomfield calls 'phonetic alternants', because the choice among them is determined by phonotactic rules of English that require agreement in voicing between obstruents at the end of a word, and forbid a sequence of two sibilants in that position. But not all English plural forms can be described in these terms. Take, for instance, those nouns where the singular ends in an unvoiced fricative which is voiced in the plural (e.g. *knife* [nɑɪf] – *knives* [nɑɪvz], *mouth* [maʊθ] – *mouths* [maʊðz], *house* [haʊs] – *houses* [haʊzɪz]):

> We can describe the peculiarity of these plurals by saying that the final [f,θ,s] of the underlying singular is replaced by [v,ð,z] before the bound form is added. The word 'before' in this statement means that the alternant of the bound form is the one appropriate to the substituted sound; thus the plural of *knife* adds not [-s] but [-z]: 'first' the [-f] is replaced by [-v] and then the appropriate alternant [-z] is added. The terms 'before, after, first, then', and so on, in such statements, tell the *descriptive order*. The actual sequence of constituents and their structural order are a part of the language, but the descriptive order of grammatical features is a fiction and results simply from our method of describing the forms; it goes without saying, for instance, that the speaker who says *knives* does not 'first' replace [f] by [v] and 'then' add [-z], but merely utters a form (*knives*) which in certain features resembles and in certain features differs from a certain other form (namely, *knife*).
>
> (Bloomfield 1935: 213)

Another irregular English plural is *oxen*. Here the *-en* is a 'suppletive alternant' of the plural morpheme: there is no other noun in the language which does precisely this to form its plural, and there is no phonetic explanation of its occurrence. A survey of the plurals of English nouns also offers cases of 'zero-alternants' (*sheep – sheep*, etc.), where there is no overt indication of plurality at all. Bloomfield also allows for 'substitution-alternants':

> the plural nouns *geese, feet, teeth, mice, lice, men, women* . . . add no bound form to the singular, but contain a different syllabic. In these plurals a grammatical feature, phonetic modification, expresses a meaning (namely, . . . *'more than one object'*) which is normally expressed by a linguistic form (namely, the morpheme [-ez, -z, -s]. We may say that 'substitution of [ij]' (for the stressed syllabic of the underlying form) in *geese, teeth, feet*, 'substitution of [aj]' in *mice, lice*, 'substitution of [e]' in *men* and 'substitution of [i]' in *women*, are alternants of the normal plural-suffix.
>
> (Bloomfield 1935: 216)

Does Bloomfield's definition of the morpheme as 'a form which bears no partial phonetic-semantic resemblance to any other form' provide an operational guide to the pleromatic analysis of a language? An affirmative answer to this is hindered by the difficulty of understanding what he means both by 'form' and by 'phonetic-semantic resemblance'.

[ʤanfɛl], we are told, contains more than one morpheme, because parts of it bear a phonetic-semantic resemblance to parts of other utterances. The first three segments resemble those of [ʤanɹæn], and the last three those of [dænfɛl]. Therefore, *John* and *fell* are two separate morphemes. But what needs clarifying is why the analysis should stop there. For the comparison of *John* with *Dan* suggests a partial phonetic-semantic resemblance which Bloomfield has overlooked. Both are men's names, and both end in *-n*. Other names, such as *Ben, Len, Ken, Don, Jan, Ron, Win*, suggest that the analysis should isolate a simple form *-n*, and that all such names are bimorphemic. It is true that one has great difficulty in stating just what the 'constant meaning' that morphemes are supposed to have might be in the case of *-n*. But this is not a consideration that ought to worry Bloomfield, at least if his practice in other cases is anything to go by. If failure to specify its presumed constant meaning were a bar to recognizing a morpheme, there would be no justification for a bimorphemic analysis of, for example, *cranberry*. For Bloomfield is quite unable to show that the *cran-* of *cranberry* has

61

any meaning at all, let alone that that meaning is 'constant'. The argument for counting *cran-* as a morpheme is merely that cranberries 'are a definite kind of berry'. Now it is true that the presence of *cran-* in the frame —— *-berry* tells us that we are talking of cranberries. But it does not follow from that that the element *cran-* means 'whatever distinguishes cranberries from other kinds of berry'. It might similarly be said that it is the presence of *mon-* in the frame —— *-goose* that tells us that we are talking of mongooses rather than geese. But we would not for that reason be tempted to say that the meaning of *mon-* is whatever distinguishes mongooses from geese. It might be objected that the comparison is inapposite, in that whereas a cranberry is a kind of berry, a mongoose is not a kind of goose. But this point, though true, would be irrelevant. A shaman is a kind of man. But this would not be taken to justify a bimorphemic analysis of *shaman*.

The suspicion that Bloomfield does not take his own definition of the morpheme seriously is reinforced when we consider the case of words like (a) *perceive, pertain, deceive, detain*, and, conversely, words like (b) *no, not, none, never, neither*.

Perceive, pertain, deceive, detain are each analysed as bimorphemic, the morphemes in question being *per-*, *de-*, *-ceive* and *-tain*. The problem is that no attempt is made to state what the meaning of any of these elements is. If *per-* is a morpheme found in the initial syllable of *perceive* and *pertain*, then we are presumably invited to believe that adding *per-* to *-tain* modifies its meaning in the same way that adding *per-* to *-ceive* modifies the meaning of *-ceive*. But since it is hard to see what the meanings of *-ceive* and *-tain* are supposed to be anyway, this fails to convince.

The converse objection applies to Bloomfield's treatment of the words of (b). For here it seems clear that we have to do in each case with an initial morpheme *n-*, meaning, we might say, 'negative'. Bloomfield says about these words (1935: 244) that 'here we find clearly marked phonetic-semantic resemblances between elements which we view as different roots'. But it is precisely because there are clearly marked phonetic-semantic resemblances that these words should, according to the definition, be viewed as containing the same root.

Sometimes Bloomfield insists on a bimorphemic analysis where it is hard to see any justification for treating the forms concerned as other than monomorphemic. In other cases he treats as monomorphemic forms which appear to be complex. Alongside these there is a third class, exemplified by the word *spider*, where he is quite equivocal as to the correct treatment:

> *Primary words* contain no free forms among their immediate constituents. They may be *complex*, consisting of two or more bound forms, as *per-ceive, per-tain, con-ceive, de-tain*, or they may be simple, as *boy, run, red, and, in, ouch*. The bound forms which make up complex primary words are determined, of course, by features of partial resemblance, as in the examples just cited. In many languages, the primary words show a structural resemblance to secondary words. Thus in English the primary words *hammer, rudder, spider* resemble secondary words like *dancer, leader, writer* . . . Primary affixes may be extremely vague in meaning and act merely as an obligatory accompaniment (a *determinative*) of the root. In English, the commonest primary suffixes do not even tell the part of speech; thus we have, with *-er, spider, bitter, linger, ever, under*; with *-le, bottle, little, hustle*; with *-ow, furrow, yellow, borrow* . . .
> (Bloomfield 1935: 240–1)

Anyone who wants to know whether *spider* is morphemically *spider* or *spid-er* will have to make what he can of the statement that the *-er* of *spider* is an affix (which appears to suggest that the word is bimorphemic), in conjunction with the statement that 'primary affixes are extremely vague in meaning and act merely as an obligatory accompaniment of the root' (which appears to suggest that the 'affix' is not independently meaningful and therefore that *spider* is a single morpheme).

It seems that a definition of the morpheme based on the presence or absence of phonetic-semantic resemblances is in practice quite inoperable. Moreover it is in any case unclear what Bloomfield means by a 'form'. It seemed at the outset of his exposition that a form was an isolable linear sequence of sounds in an utterance. But the subsequent admission into the analysis of various kinds of 'alternant' casts doubt on this. If we are to treat the *-en* of *oxen* and the *-s* of *cats* as variants of one and the same form, then 'forms' are not after all identifiable elements of surface structure, but something more abstract. In cases like *mouse/mice*, it is doubtful whether we can reasonably talk of a form at all, since the plural 'form' here is the operation of substituting one vowel for another. Here the 'fiction' resulting 'from our method of describing the forms' seems to have been confused with the forms themselves.

A further problem with these 'alternants' is that they consort ill with Bloomfield's assertion that 'we suppose . . . that there are no actual synonyms' (1935: 145). If -*en* and -*s* are to be taken as alternants of one morpheme, this cannot be because of any similarity between them in respect of form, for there is none. It must, therefore, be because of a similarity in respect of meaning. -*s* and -*en* are alternants of the same morpheme because they both mean 'more than one'. That is, they are synonymous. It might be counter-argued that there is no inconsistency here, in that it is precisely in order to avoid treating -*s* and -*en* as different synonymous forms that they are counted as alternants of the same form. But this cannot be the case, as Bloomfield explicitly states that 'if the forms are phonemically different, we suppose that their meanings are different'. -*s* and -*en* are phonemically different, but far from supposing that their meanings are different, it is in virtue of being able to suppose that their meanings are the same that we recognize them as alternants of one morpheme. It is hard to exculpate Bloomfield from a charge of confusing two very different concepts of 'form', and, on that basis, of advocating a concept of the morpheme that is in practice quite unworkable.

Some of the difficulties illustrated here are not intrinsic to any attempt to identify a set of pleremes, but peculiar to Bloomfield. Saussure, for example, does not confuse different senses of 'form': for him, -*en* and -*s* are different 'signs'. Nonetheless Bloomfield's account has one salient feature characteristic of attempts to define a minimal unit of form. Despite the proliferation of neologistic terminology and for all the analytical sophistication he brings to bear on the problem, he would have done at least as well simply to claim at the outset, just as Firth does, that we already know how to analyse utterances into their constituent pleremes. His definition of the morpheme is not a discovery procedure which when brought to bear on a language yields the relevant analysis. Bloomfield takes it that he already knows, in a rough and ready way, what the morphemes of English are: the definition is a retrospective attempt to characterize that knowledge. Where the definition fails to fit, it is jettisoned. The idea that a language *must* consist of an identifiable set of pleremes is so far taken for granted that any difficulty in showing, in terms of a given definition, what the set comprises can only cast doubt on the definition, not on the idea that there is such a set. That of course is because, if communication by means of language really is a matter of encoding and decoding messages, such a set must be recoverable.

As far as general linguistic theory is concerned, the main point of the closed circle of ideas just outlined is that it underwrites the preoccupation of linguists with the synchronic description of fixed, monolithic systems of form-meaning correspondences called 'languages', and hence provides the basis for a would-be science of spoken language in all essentials continuous with the western tradition of grammatical inquiry. But, because this circle of ideas is taken as fundamental to our grasp of what languages are and how they function, the linguistic science erected upon it claims to shed light on topics quite other than the mere grammatical description of languages. Its ramifications and consequences are far-reaching. In the next two sections of this chapter it is proposed to consider the distortions it introduces into the study of (i) language acquisition and (ii) linguistic variation.

II

The theorist primarily responsible for the idea that linguistics should be concerned with language acquisition is Chomsky. Chomsky's linguistics is one specific version of the psycho-biological interpretation of generativism. Broadly speaking, to interpret generativist linguistics psycho-biologically is to suppose that the writing of generative grammars, and the study of generative grammatical theory, are relevant to an attempt to distinguish those aspects of the general phenomenon called 'language' which fall within the province of the natural sciences from those which do not. Equipping us with the capacity for language is perhaps biology's chief contribution to human culture, and it would therefore be interesting to understand just how, in what respects, and to what extent language is determined by our biological nature. More narrowly, Chomsky is particularly concerned with psycho-biological generativism as an approach to the question of how children acquire their native language.

The starting-point for this inquiry is the proposition that no matter what linguistic community they are brought up in, all physically and psychologically normal children develop unconscious knowledge of, and hence the ability to utter and comprehend, the infinitely large set of spoken sentences which constitutes the language in question. This ability is achieved despite the fact that the experiential basis for doing so (the 'stimulus') is in various respects deficient. Deficiencies of the stimulus fall into two main categories: 'degeneracy' and 'poverty'. Here we will focus on poverty.

The stimulus is impoverished in that although a child comes eventually to be able to deal with an infinite range of sentences of his language, he directly encounters only a finite sample of them. Yet as a mature speaker he has no more difficulty in producing and understanding sentences he has never heard before than he has in dealing with those that have actually figured in his past linguistic experience. Moreover, it is not just that he deals effortlessly with new sentences as such. He will also somehow come to know that well-formed sentences of previously unencountered grammatical types are legitimate and acceptable. Conversely, children are not systematically informed as to the illegitimacy of certain logically possible but non-occurrent sentence-types, but nonetheless never produce sentences of such types. In recent generativist writings illustrations of this latter phenomenon tend to turn on the grammatical vagaries of either the English phrase *each other* or else of the formation of *wh*-questions. Berwick and Weinberg, for instance, offer (1984: 18–19) the following example. In a sentence such as *Ronald Reagan finally issued a statement without contradicting it*, the final pronoun *it*, they observe, 'co-refers with' the object of the verb, *a statement*. One can formulate a similar sentence where the final pronoun stands for the subject: *Ronald Reagan finally issued a statement without contradicting himself*. Both subject and object of the first part of these sentences may be questioned, as in *Who finally issued a statement?* and *Which statement did Ronald Reagan finally issue?* But if similar questions are formed corresponding to the original full sentences, a divergence arises between the treatment of subject and object: although *Which statement did Ronald Reagan finally issue without contradicting?* (where *it* is omitted at the end) is grammatical, **Who finally issued a statement without contradicting?* (where *himself* is omitted at the end) is not. The point is that there is no obvious reason for this lacuna in the inventory of possible English sentence-types; and its impossibility is not explicitly taught to apprentice English-speakers. But all mature English-speakers unconsciously know that sentences of that kind are ungrammatical. Likewise, speakers know, without ever having had it overtly pointed out to them, that a given sentence of their language is ambiguous, or that certain sets of sentences are paraphrases of one another. In short, speakers come to have unconscious knowledge of the structure and organization of their language, for at least some parts of which there is no direct evidence available in the data they are exposed to as children.

The poverty of the stimulus, in Chomsky's view, reveals the kind of phenomenon first-language acquisition is. How can the mature speaker eventually have linguistic knowledge for which his direct experience as a child provides no warrant? Moreover, despite variation among individuals as to background and intelligence, their mature linguistic capacity emerges in a fairly uniform fashion, in just a few years, without much apparent effort, conscious thought, or difficulty; and during its development only a narrow range of the logically possible errors are ever made. Children do not test random hypotheses, gradually discarding those leading to 'incorrect' results. On the contrary, the ill-formed sentences produced by young children seem to be few in type and rather uniform from one child to another. Despite the poverty of the stimulus, normal children attain a rich system of linguistic knowledge by five or six years of age, and a mature system by the time of puberty. Such a feat can only be possible on the basis that certain things about the language they are learning are known a priori, in the sense that they are somehow available to them irrespective of their idiosyncratically deficient linguistic experience. Furthermore, this a priori knowledge cannot be knowledge pertaining to the structure of particular languages, since children master whatever language they happen to be exposed to in infancy.

What is proposed, therefore, is that certain abstract principles pertaining to the grammatical structure of all languages (that is, of human language in general), are genetically encoded in the brain. Children come into the world already primed to acquire a language of a certain logically rather arbitrarily delimited type. It will be a particular species of the genus 'human language', whose general organizational principles are universal, determined by our common genetic inheritance. The unfailing ease and accuracy with which children acquire their language is to be explained by supposing that the inadequate and fragmentary evidence as to its structure available to them empirically is supplemented by a system of innately known universal organizational principles.

Chomsky insists that the gap between the empirically available evidence and the linguistic knowledge of the mature speaker cannot be bridged by (appeal to) any general mechanisms or processes of learning. This view he bases on considerations such as the following:

> There are, in fact, striking and obvious differences between language learning and the learning (or discovery) of physics. In the first case, a rich and complex system of rules is attained in a uniform way, rapidly, effortlessly, on the basis of limited and rather degenerate evidence. In the second case, we are forced to proceed on the basis of consciously articulated principles subjected to careful verification with the intervention of individual insight and often genius. It is clear enough that the cognitive domains in question are quite different. Humans are designed to learn language, which is nothing other than what their minds construct when placed in appropriate conditions: they are not designed in anything like the same way to learn physics. Gross observations suffice to suggest that very different principles of 'learning' are involved.
>
> (Chomsky 1983: 320)

Indeed, it is questionable whether 'learning' is a useful notion at all where language acquisition is concerned: we are dealing, rather, with the growth and eventual maturation, under environmental stimulus, of a 'mental organ'. In this view, we no more 'learn' our native language than ovaries 'learn' to shed eggs. In fact, 'it is possible that the notion "learning" may go the way of the rising and setting of the sun' (Chomsky 1980: 139).

So human beings must be equipped with a distinct 'language faculty', providing them from the outset with what is sometimes referred to as a 'general theory of grammar'. This represents the genetic equipment that facilitates language acquisition and delimits the linguistic knowledge that will eventually be attained via the interaction of the language faculty with the evidence available to the child as to the forms and structures of the particular language he is acquiring.

The aspect of linguistic structure with which most generativists are centrally concerned is syntax. As far as the syntactic aspect of language is concerned, Chomsky nowadays characterizes the initial state of the language faculty as a system of 'fundamental principles', many of which have 'open parameters' associated with them. Subjacency, for instance, is the principle that a phrase cannot be moved too far within a sentence, where 'too far' means 'beyond the limits of two bounding categories'. As a fundamental principle, subjacency is in Chomsky's view genetically encoded. However, a principle such as subjacency may have one or more open parameters whose values are fixed by the child's linguistic experience. For instance, English and Italian both exhibit subjacency, but they differ in regard to the way in which the choice of bounding category is fixed. The important point here is how this distinction between fundamental principles and open parameters relates to the general question of language acquisition. It provides the basis for an account of how it is possible for the initial state of the language faculty to satisfy two apparently conflicting conditions. On the one hand, the initial state must be sufficiently accommodating for it to be possible in principle for the child to acquire any one of the wide variety of structurally different human languages. On the other hand, it must be sufficiently restrictive for it to be possible for the child to acquire, on the basis of limited evidence, the specific language of the speech community to which he belongs. The genetically determined fundamental principles provide for the plasticity to acquire any language, while the open parameters make it possible to acquire some specific language, by a process of 'fixing the parameters' on the basis of linguistic experience.

There are various reasons why it is questionable to what extent these ideas add up to a theory of language acquisition. These have to do with various idealizations on which the theorizing is based. But before discussing these idealizations it is necessary to draw attention to Chomsky's concept of a language.

Chomsky is not – at least, not in theory – concerned with languages as institutionalized cultural products: that is, with entities such as those we call 'English' or 'French' or 'German', as discussed, inventoried and analysed by philologists, lexicographers, grammarians, etc. In the latest terminology such entities are examples of 'E[xternalized]-languages', and contrasted with 'I[nternalized]-languages'. The essence of the distinction is that whereas, as Botha puts it (1987: 76), 'an E-language is an object that exists outside the mind of a speaker-listener', an I-language 'is some element of the mind of the person who knows the language, acquired by the learner, and used by the speaker-hearer' (Chomsky 1986: 22). That is, an I-language is a native speaker's linguistic knowledge, or internalized grammar.[7] So it is not native-speaker acquisition of 'English', 'French', etc. as the layman knows them that Chomsky is concerned with. Languages, in this sense, are no more than by-products of the externalization or implementation of an I-language, a process which in any case involves the interaction of the language faculty with many other departments of the mind.

But there is a strange twist here. It is not just that Chomsky's theory is uninterested in accounting for the acquisition of what most people are likely to think of as 'languages'. His theory may not be directly concerned with languages in that sense, but many of them are at least allowed for by the theory, so far as they are seen as a sort of collective precipitation thrown up by the use of the I-languages of the speaker-listeners in a particular speech-community. But there are some languages which do not appear to have even this status. That is, there are languages which are apparently not to be envisaged as the product of a large number of different but similar 'underlying' I-languages, because they are 'impure'; and Chomsky's theory is exclusively concerned with what he calls 'pure' languages (Chomsky 1986: 17). So speakers of impure languages are, presumably, either held not to have I-languages, or else their I-languages and the acquisition of them lie outside the domain of Chomsky's investigation. And the twist is that the boundary between pure and impure languages appears to correspond roughly to the boundary between languages which do, and languages which for one or another reason do not, fall within the purview of the traditional grammarian, philologist, etc.

Chomsky's example of an impure language is the mixture of Russian and French spoken by some members of the nineteenth-century Russian aristocracy. It is not entirely clear what general idea this example is intended to illustrate,[8] but it is clear enough that such a mixture would not be the object of a traditional grammarian's attention. Roughly speaking, the traditional grammarian is concerned, first, with the literary languages of classical antiquity; second, with the standardized 'official' languages of the nation-states of post-Renaissance Europe; and thirdly, with any other languages similar to these in being culturally prestigious and having given rise to a more or less stable written form (preferably enshrined in literary works of acknowledged merit), so that 'speaking the language correctly' may be represented, for all practical (e.g. pedagogical) purposes, as implementing that form (or something very close to it) in the oro-aural dimension. If this is what a pure language is, then clearly Russian and French, for instance, would qualify as pure languages, while a mixture of

Russian and French would not. Nor, presumably, would most pidgins and creoles, which are, at least in the traditional view, highly unstable 'jargons' arising in anomalous circumstances and for the most part lacking cultural authority.

Of more equivocal status are dying languages, such as Welsh. Welsh has of course been, and still is, an object of traditional grammatical inquiry. But it is questionable whether the contemporary spoken language can be viewed, in the usual way, as an oro-aural manifestation of that object. The first problem with Welsh, in this context, is to decide who counts as a 'speaker'. Monolingual Welsh-speakers are thin on the ground these days, and tend to be either under four years old or over eighty. Most Welsh-speakers are bilingual in English, and their Welsh is to varying degrees contaminated by English. Welsh contains an enormous number of lexical borrowings from English. Many of these are of long standing, and established as part of any Welsh-speaker's vocabulary. But the fact that the native Welsh vocabulary is radically deficient in the words required for talking about virtually any aspect of life specifically characteristic of the twentieth century gives rise to a penumbral area where it is difficult to decide whether we are dealing with the use of a non-native but nonetheless Welsh word or construction, or a lapse into English. Welshmen, when speaking Welsh, use words like *wage-freeze*, *hamburger*, *fridge*, and in writing they may spell them according to Welsh conventions (e.g. *ffrij*), but it is unclear whether we should count them as Welsh words.

There are also more complex kinds of English influence, affecting grammar as well as vocabulary. Here are some, not at all far-fetched,[9] examples of contemporary 'Welsh' expressions: *mae'r rhain wedi catchio on* 'these have caught on', *mae hi wedi committio suicide* 'she has committed suicide', *mi na'th o chickenio allan* 'he chickened out', *mae'r ducks yn swimio ar y water* 'the ducks are swimming on the water' (*-io* is an infinitive verb ending; *allan* means 'out'; all the obviously English words and phrases here, such as *catch on*, *swim*, *water*, etc. have native Welsh equivalents). Such *ad hoc* improvisations are characteristic of 'semi-speakers' of a dying language: those for whom interference from language B has reached the point where their grasp of language A, even if it is their mother tongue, is no better than that of a not very efficient second-language learner. Not all Welsh speakers would say such things, and not all of those who say them sometimes would always do so: some also control what Chomsky might be inclined to see as a 'purer' Welsh for use on more formal occasions. But there are certain lexical subsystems where substitution of English expressions is quite general. Many Welsh speakers invariably use the English words for the months of the year (but not, for some reason, the days of the week). Common, too, is the use of *left* and *right*, and English numerals: *mae hi'n byw yma ers twenty-two years* 'she has lived here for twenty-two years', *mae'r car 'ma yn gneud thirty miles i'r galwyn* 'this car does thirty miles to the gallon'. This leads to the time being told in English: *mae'r bws yn mynd o'r pentre twenty-five to six* 'the bus goes from the village at twenty-five to six'.

Welsh-speakers (whoever we decide they are exactly) can be presumed to differ in respect of their attitude to such 'sentences' of their language. At one end of the spectrum we have those who would be disinclined to count any of the expressions quoted here as Welsh at all. At the other end, there are those for whom an unstable mixture of English and Welsh phrases is all the Welsh they know. In between there are those who have, to varying degrees, the ability to shift among more or less decomposed forms of the language. And almost all speakers, whatever the state of their Welsh, are fluent in English. In so far as this complex state of affairs suffices to render Welsh 'impure', (many) Welsh-speakers, we must assume, are simply not persons to whom Chomsky's theory of language acquisition is intended to apply. And that is very peculiar. For no general reason is offered for the exclusion of speakers of impure languages from the domain of the theory.

A different idealization of the acquisition process arises from a distinction between what are known as the 'logical' and the 'psychological' problems of language acquisition. The logical problem is essentially that of explaining in general terms how it can in principle be possible for children, on the basis of partial and deficient exposure to their language, to acquire the complex and rich system that constitutes their mature linguistic knowledge. The 'psychological' problem, in contrast, is the problem of 'real-time' acquisition: what does the actual process of acquiring a language consist in? Chomsky does not seek an answer to this latter question; and concentration on the 'logical' problem to the exclusion of the 'psychological' problem implies that certain kinds of evidence which might prima facie be thought to have a bearing on the question of acquisition are automatically discounted as irrelevant. For instance, the data constituted by the various kinds of distorted, simplified, or otherwise ungrammatical utterances produced by children at various stages in the process of acquiring their language are presumably available to children themselves, and are, no doubt, 'input' to a subsequent stage of the 'real-time' acquisition process. But since the real-time acquisition process is not what is at issue, such utterances are excluded from consideration. In other words, Chomsky assumes for theoretical purposes that acquisition is instantaneous: he is concerned with the general question of what in principle is required if the gap between available linguistic evidence and mature linguistic knowledge is to be bridged, and not with the question of how in practice the bridge is actually built.

This is a curious theoretical compromise. We can, however, see how it is forced on Chomsky. On the one hand, real-world speakers and speech-events must come into the story somewhere, otherwise the 'logical problem', as posed, would vanish. It is a gap that the initial state of the language faculty fills, not a void. But on the other hand, real-world speakers and real-time speech-events must not be given a role so large that they might conceivably abolish the gap altogether. Acquisition must not be assimilable to learning.

Some may find it difficult to see why any eventual solution to the 'logical problem', as thus conceived, should be treated as having any bearing on language acquisition in the real world. Not only is the compromise between completely idealized and genuinely real-world acquisition theoretically unsatisfactory, but the questions which the theory is designed to answer in any case seem largely spurious.

For instance, the query 'how do children come to master an infinitely large set of spoken sentences?' is vulnerable to two observations. First, it is far from clear what a 'spoken sentence' is, and hence even less clear that a spoken language is properly envisaged as an infinite set of them. Second, even if these conceptual problems were resolved, it would remain to be demonstrated that native speakers are actually in possession of such mastery. Thus the proposition which forms the starting-point for the whole inquiry is far from securely established.

On the other hand, the claim that there is a gap between our linguistic knowledge and what we have an evidential basis for knowing is prima facie more promising, in that here we are undoubtedly faced with facts requiring explanation. But the interpretation imposed on those facts is curious. It is a fact, for instance, that most English-speakers (that is, most speakers of I-languages which might be associated with the concept 'English') are unlikely to produce utterances like 'Who finally issued a statement without contradicting?', and a further fact that there is nothing in what English-speakers do say from which an apprentice English-speaker could readily infer the relevant grammatical proscription. But what the relevant grammatical proscription is, in any particular case, is not evident from mere inspection of the linguistic expression (or non-expression) held to exemplify it. As far as this particular example is concerned, we are invited to see the tip of an iceberg of language-faculty-embedded principles governing the formation of *wh*-questions. But there is at least as much reason to see no more than one or other of a number of idiosyncratic facts about the verb *contradict*. One is that *contradict*, unlike its Germanic counterpart *gainsay*, is peculiar in allowing a reflexive personal object at all (compare *Ronald Reagan contradicted himself* with **Ronald Reagan gainsaid himself*). Or the relevant fact could be that *contradict*, unlike *demur*, *dissent*, and other words in the same general semantic field, is currently transitive. In this view no more would be required to make *Who finally issued a statement without contradicting?* grammatical than an inversion of the kind of change that has made *Which policies were the demonstrators protesting?* grammatical in American, but not British, English. Or, given that *contradict* is transitive, the peculiarity might be that it has so far failed to develop the kind of formally intransitive use with object implied or 'understood' which characterizes many basically transitive verbs (*he drinks*, for instance, is as grammatical as *he drinks whisky*). There is nothing ungrammatical about the sentence formed by omitting *himself* from *Who finally left the bathroom without washing himself?*; and it is hard to believe that there is some deep reason of principle why *contradict* should not develop a similar construction. It could start happening tomorrow.

There are two points here. First, it is not that the non-sentence in question cannot be seen as exemplifying the grammatical point it is held to exemplify. But whether it does so depends on the point of view adopted. And the point of view from which the non-occurrence of **Who finally issued a statement without contradicting?* demonstrates a restriction on the possible types of well-formed *wh*-question is that of the linguist concerned, precisely, to establish the general grammatical fact in question. But its non-occurrence cannot necessarily be expected to have the same significance for the speaker-listener. The fact, if it is a fact, that he 'knows' this sentence to be ungrammatical is not in itself evidence for his 'knowledge' of the underlying explanatory principle. Botha (1987: 22–3) is scornful of those who criticize generativists for assuming that the language-acquirer is a 'little linguist'. But it seems that some such assumption is inherent in the very attempt to demonstrate the existence of grammatical principles given by the initial state of the language faculty by citing what the native speaker 'cannot say'. For it is only if he adopts the linguist's point of view that the reason he cannot say it has to be seen as being the one offered.

The second point is that what requires explanation here is misinterpreted by the generativist. Granted that there is a stability of usage which allows it to be correctly said, for example, that in current English *Who finally issued a statement without contradicting?* is ungrammatical, the interesting question is how such stabilities can come about, given the circumstances in which language is actually used. What are the processes by which, out of the incessant flux of utterance, usages come to be, or at any rate to seem, at least temporarily fixed and codifiable? A satisfactory answer to this question, clarifying as it would at least one dimension of the fundamental distinction between 'language' and 'a language', would clearly be relevant to an understanding of language acquisition. But it is not a question that the generativist considers. His question is, granted that a language is a fixed system of grammatical sentences for which there is a paucity of evidence in the utterances to which the learner is exposed, how is the system nonetheless acquired? His answer to this question leads him to seek to explain, not how and why there should be stabilities at all, but the much less significant fact that the stabilities currently happen to be what they are. In short, what requires explanation is misrepresented from the outset by a priori theoretical fiat.

For these various reasons it is hard to see that there is very much to Chomsky's claim to have a theory of language acquisition. It would therefore be interesting to trace the steps by which Chomsky comes to see himself as having one.

In 1957 Chomsky published his first book, *Syntactic Structures*. In it he considers some basic theoretical requirements for the construction of a grammar, viewed as a device for generating the sentences of a language. The book contains a discussion of finite-state, phrase-structure, and transformational grammars; a detailed account of the English auxiliary system; arguments for treating syntax as independent of semantics; and many other things. What it does not contain is any hint of a suggestion that this theorizing about grammar might be relevant to the study of the mind, or to the study of how a child acquires his native language – in general, to the concern with the psycho-biological foundations of language that has latterly dominated Chomsky's linguistic thinking.

Now this is not because Chomsky had not at that stage developed his psycho-biological interests. The relevance of generative grammar to language acquisition is clearly stated in Chomsky (1975), a version of which antedates *Syntactic Structures*, and of which *Syntactic Structures* is in fact a sort of extract. Apparently Chomsky omitted any reference to the mentalistic implications of generative grammar from *Syntactic Structures* because he thought at the time that such ideas were too audacious to print. However that may be, the fact that they can be omitted from an exposition of the principles of generative grammar shows that the connection between generativism and the study of the mind (in particular, the study of acquisition) is at any rate not a necessary connection. And that observation prompts the question: what kind of connection is it? What, in other words, are the reasons for supposing that generative grammars have anything to do with language acquisition?

One plausible answer comes from a comparison of Chomsky's early work with that of his distributionalist predecessors. A distributional linguistic analysis, as explicated by Z. S. Harris (1951), attempts to state the permissible patterns of arrangement of linguistic units identified in a corpus of utterances taken, for purposes of the analysis, as representing the language as a whole. As Harris points out on the very first page of *Methods in Structural Linguistics*, he is not bothered about where the linguist gets his data from. 'It does not matter', he says, 'if the linguist obtains his data by taking texts, questioning an informant, or recording a conversation'. All that matters is that the corpus should be large enough to constitute a fair sample of the language in question, so that it may for practical purposes be assumed that no major class of constructions, utterance-types, or units of the language is unrepresented. Now Harris himself recognized that his methods of analysis, if fully worked out, can be turned round, so to speak, and used as the basis for synthesizing or predicting new utterances of the language not already in the corpus:

The work of analysis leads right up to the statements which enable anyone to synthesise or predict utterances in the language. These statements form a deductive system with axiomatically defined initial elements and with theorems concerning the relations among them. The final theorems would indicate the structure of the utterances of the language in terms of the preceding parts of the system.

(Harris 1951: 372–3)

Chomsky can be seen as having taken up his teacher's challenge to develop a formal system of axioms and deductive rules which would 'synthesise or predict' the well-formed sentences of a natural language. (Or let us be more accurate and say that Chomsky took up the challenge of considering in theoretical terms the possibility of developing such formal systems: it is worth pointing out that Chomsky himself has never actually written a generative grammar or even a considerable fragment of one.)[10]

The emphasis on synthesis rather than analysis naturally leads Chomsky to play up the inadequacies of a corpus-based approach and to stress the open-endedness of natural languages. And it is here we see Chomsky first opening the way to insinuating that the grammatical preoccupations of linguists might be interpreted as a psycho-biological inquiry into language as a mental phenomenon generally, and into language acquisition in particular. For we note a certain rhetorical exaggeration in Chomsky's early pronouncements about the inadequacies of the language-as-corpus view. He sometimes writes as though American descriptivists and distributionalists from the 1930s onwards mistakenly believed that languages just *were* collections of antecedently given data. Bloomfield, Harris, *et al.* believed nothing of the kind: if they treated languages as fixed corpora, that is because it was procedurally convenient, not because in doing so they captured the essence of what languages are 'really like'. So we can see from Chomsky's dismissive remarks about so-called 'structural' linguistics that in taking up Harris's challenge to move from analysis to synthesis in grammatical description he perceived an opportunity to link up the study of grammar with a range of interesting questions about what languages are for their speakers. The psychologistic concerns of Saussurean structuralism, which had been banished from American linguistics in the intervening period, were now to be readmitted.

It is obvious enough that for anyone who wants his linguistic descriptions to be 'psychologically real', it is no good starting from the idea of a language as a pre-existing corpus of sentences which requires analysis. This cannot possibly be what a natural language is for the native speaker-hearer, whether adult or mere apprentice. But the idea of a language as an indefinitely large potential corpus of sentences which requires synthesis is much more promising. It appears to capture an essential feature of the language-user's experience: that he is incessantly confronted with the need to produce and understand expressions which he has never encountered before. And the first hint we have in a book by Chomsky that generative grammars may be more than just grammars lays stress on this point:

> The central fact to which any significant linguistic theory must address itself to is this: a mature speaker can produce a new sentence of his language on the appropriate occasion, and other speakers can understand it immediately, though it is equally new to them. Most of our linguistic experience, both as speakers and hearers, is with new sentences; once we have mastered a language, the class of sentences with which we can operate fluently and without difficulty or hesitation is so vast that for all practical purposes . . . we can regard it as infinite. Normal mastery of a language involves not only the ability to understand immediately an indefinite number of entirely new sentences, but also the ability to identify deviant sentences and, on occasion, to impose an interpretation on them . . . On the basis of a limited experience with the data of speech, each normal human has developed for himself a thorough competence in his native language. This competence can be represented, to an as yet undetermined extent, as a system of rules that we can call the *grammar* of his language.
>
> (Chomsky 1964: 7–9)

So what is involved here is a simple analogy: between the linguist's task of attempting an exhaustive description of a language which consists of indefinitely many sentences, and the child's task in learning such a language.

In assessing the value of this analogy it is worth bearing in mind where the idea comes from that a language should be seen as an indefinitely large set of sentences. It is not an idea about what a language is that is likely to be entertained by the average lay language-user. If you ask the man in the street to tell you what he thinks a language is, no doubt you will get a very wide range of answers (if you get a coherent answer at all). But one that is not likely to be forthcoming is the answer that a language is an indefinitely large set of sentences generated by the unconsciously known rules of a 'grammar'. In linguistics, as Saussure pointed out (1922: 23), it is the point of view that creates the object. And the point of view from which *that* is a good answer to the question 'what is a language?' is the point of view of a linguist interested in introducing a certain kind of mathematical model as a basis for his linguistic descriptions.

This is not to deny that Chomsky is free to define a language as the set of sentences generated by the rules of a grammar, if he likes. But it is important to bear in mind that when Chomsky claims to have a theory of language acquisition, he is talking, not about languages 'as we know them', but about abstract entities which he has stipulatively defined in order to create a domain within which to manipulate certain descriptive procedures. The analogy between the linguist's task and the child's will be unconvincing to anyone who fails to see why what a generative grammarian calls 'a language' should be treated, without further argument or discussion, as the thing that a child is acquiring. There is a passage near the beginning of Chomsky 1975 which brings out very clearly the rhetorical trick or terminological obfuscation involved here. In the formulation given in that book, an explanatorily adequate general linguistic theory is:

> a theory of the innate, intrinsic language faculty that provides the basis for the acquisition of knowledge of language. The child, in his 'initial state' is uninformed as to the language of the speech community in which he lives. Plainly, he is endowed with some set of mechanisms (what we may call his 'language faculty') for determining this language, that is, for achieving a final state in which he knows the language. General linguistic theory describes his initial state, the grammar of his language describes his final state.
>
> (Chomsky 1975: 9)

Immediately before the passage just quoted, Chomsky has defined a language *L* as 'a set, in general infinite, of finite strings of symbols drawn from a finite alphabet'. But in the above quotation Chomsky slips from talking of *L*, as thus defined, into using the everyday term 'language'. The reason for this is clear enough if we reword the quotation, substituting for the phrase 'a language' Chomsky's own definition of the term. Now the passage runs as follows:

> The child, in his initial state is uninformed as to the set of finite strings of symbols drawn from a finite vocabulary of the speech community in which he lives. Plainly, he is endowed with some set of mechanisms (what we may call his 'language faculty') for determining this set of finite strings of symbols, that is, for achieving a final state in which he knows the set of finite strings of symbols. General linguistic theory describes his initial state, the grammar of his set of strings of symbols describes his final state.

Such a substitution would raise all too acutely the question why we should suppose that what a child acquires, in learning his native language, is knowledge of a set of strings of symbols.

In more recent work Chomsky has overtly discussed certain difficulties surrounding the concept of a language. For instance, in *Rules and Representations* (1980) we find the following much-quoted statement:

> If the study of human language is to be pursued in a serious way, it is necessary to undertake a series of abstractions and idealizations. Consider the concept 'language' itself. The term is hardly clear; 'language' is no well-defined concept of linguistic science. In colloquial usage we say that German is one language and Dutch another, but some dialects of German are more similar to Dutch dialects than to other, more remote dialects of German. We say that Chinese is a language with many dialects, and that French, Italian and Spanish are different languages. But the diversity of the Chinese 'dialects' is roughly comparable to that of the Romance languages. A linguist knowing nothing about political boundaries or institutions would not distinguish 'language' and 'dialect' as we do in normal discourse. Nor would he have any clear alternative concepts to propose, with anything like the same function . . .
>
> (Chomsky 1980: 217)

So here Chomsky concedes that his theorizing is not about languages as we know them, but about objects abstracted from linguistic reality and presented as 'idealized' languages. Still more recently, he has drawn the distinction mentioned earlier between 'externalized' or E-languages, and 'internalized' or I-languages. An E-language appears to be the kind of thing discussed, up till then, by practically all grammarians, linguists, and psychologists, including Chomsky. A linguist is talking about E-languages to the extent that he views a language 'as a collection of actions, or utterances, or linguistic forms (words, sentences) paired with meanings, or as a system of linguistic forms or events' (Chomsky 1986: 19). A language thus conceived is an E-language because the 'construct is understood independently of the properties of the mind/brain'. So English, for instance, as discussed in *Syntactic Structures*, would be an E-language. Chomsky's essential point is that for a theorist who adopts an externalized concept of a language, attention is focused on the language itself. Given such an approach, 'grammar', Chomsky says, 'is a derivative notion: the linguist is free to select the grammar one way or another as long as it correctly identifies the E-language' (1986: 20). In contrast, an I-language is a system of tacit linguistic knowledge in the mind/brain of the individual. It is a state of the language faculty. Its connection with any particular concept of a given E-language is tenuous. Thus English, as an E-language, might be conceived of in various ways. It might be thought of as the total set of sentences in all the books printed in English to be found in some library. Or it might be thought of as the total set of strings of English words which a native speaker of English in 1989 would judge to be 'acceptable'. Or one might have some altogether vaguer conception of English. The point is that no such conception is of interest to the theorist concerned with I-languages. The I-language of a native English speaker (that is, the current state of his language faculty), will no doubt *help to determine* particular concepts of English as an E-language – along with many other factors, including the state of other faculties of English-speakers' minds, various kinds of cultural conditioning, and so forth. But an I-language is not to be equated with any E-language; and it is I-languages, and their acquisition, that Chomsky is now concerned with.

These more recent theoretical discussions are helpful in making it clear that anyone who expects from Chomsky a theory of how a child acquires his language, meaning by 'his language' an E-language of some kind, is going to be disappointed. In particular, if when we ask about language acquisition we have in mind, broadly, everything involved in the passage from neonatal languagelessness to becoming a competent participating member of a linguistic community, Chomsky has now made it amply clear that his theorizing is at best an attempt to understand just one of the factors involved. A competent participating member of a linguistic community brings into play a complex mosaic of knowledge and abilities of various kinds, most of which lie outside the domain of Chomsky's theory. Nonetheless, the question remains whether the 'language faculty', as identified by Chomsky, is in fact part of that complex mosaic. Chomsky has responded to critics who complain that when *he* talks about acquiring a language he is not talking about the same thing as the layman or interested observer by saying, in effect, 'indeed not'. But the observer's question was really whether the idealized, theoretical object which Chomsky used to call 'a language' has any bearing at all on 'languages' in the layman's sense. After all, it is languages in that sense that we are all of us, including Chomsky, ultimately interested in talking about. Chomsky's claim must be that it is a contribution to talking about languages in that sense to postulate a language faculty that grows in the mind, eventually reaching a final state where it consists of unconscious knowledge of an I-language which is brought into play as a necessary if not sufficient component of the mental abilities underlying a mature language-user's linguistic activities, and which it is the job of a linguist to model in a generative grammar. But whether there is such a thing at all remains questionable. For despite all the shifts of emphasis, terminological changes, and so forth, the thing which a generative grammar models obstinately retains its status as an abstraction which is only really conceivable against the background of the western grammatical tradition. That tradition arose out of, *inter alia*, a concern to teach pupils to write the languages of classical antiquity 'correctly' (that is, in imitation of acknowledged literary masters). It is easy to see how such a tradition should foster the notion that a language consists of a fixed and in principle exhaustively describable system of meaningful forms. This way of apprehending languages is firmly enshrined in western culture: we have come to think of languages as consisting of a vocabulary (listed in a dictionary), plus a set of rules (laid out in a grammar-book) for combining items from the vocabulary to form sentences; and it is on this basis, essentially, that foreign languages are still taught in our schools today. The trouble with pressing a thinly disguised version of this concept into service as the foundation for a linguistic *science* is that, far from reflecting a culture-neutral, objectively discernible fact about what languages are, it is manifestly no more than a useful way of conceiving of languages for a particular kind of pedagogical purpose.

What is more, it is virtually impossible even to state Chomsky's theory of language acquisition clearly without becoming ensnared in a conceptual incoherence. What a child acquires, according to the theory, is an I-language. His I-language is his own, unique idiolect. Nonetheless, what is seen as calling for explanation where the process of acquiring an I-language is concerned is the child's ability, given the inadequacy of the 'evidence', to achieve a swift and error-free mastery of the language of his community. But what is this community language? For the community, presumably, consists of nothing but particular individuals, whose linguistic output reflects their particular idiosyncratic idiolects. On the face of it, the theory has no room for a community language over and above the aggregate of its members' idiolects, except as a cultural construct erected via retrospective analysis of I-language-controlled linguistic output. Having taken that in, however, we have to understand that the community language somehow comes into the picture after all. For it sets the target at which the child is held to be aiming with the inadequate weapons provided by real-world experience; and it is into the gap between the power of the weapons and what they are called upon to achieve that Chomsky rhetorically inserts the need to postulate a distinct language faculty. One can only tell that the child has succeeded in learning his language, let alone be amazed at how rapidly and efficiently he has done so, if one has some yardstick against which to measure his achievement. That yardstick is the language of his community. In other words, the Chomskyan concept of an internalized I-language seems to be inextricably tangled up with 'some pretheoretical (or alternative theoretical) sense [of the notion of "a language"] . . . unavoidably present but not theoretically allowed for' (Pateman 1987: 44). Hence, among other things, the mysterious insistence that the language under description should be 'pure'. In the end, E-languages are apparently too precious to be given up. The reason Chomsky's much-trumpeted[11] impact on our ideas about the mind has been so curiously insubstantial in practice is that Chomsky's linguistics is not really about the mind at all. It is about languages, in essentially the traditional grammarian's sense. Far from being a serious attempt to investigate the psycho-biological phenomena associated with language, it is an attempt to provide a scientistic vindication of the traditional concept of languages, by projecting languages on to minds as the basis for individuals' linguistic behaviour.

What is the connection of all this with the circle of ideas outlined earlier? First, it is clear enough that Chomsky takes for granted the idea of languages as fixed codes: the various twists and turns over the years as to the details of his theorizing have left untouched the notion that a language is in principle specifiable in respect of the two dimensions of 'form' and 'meaning'. The fact that such a concept of a language answers to nothing in the observable world leads directly to the postulation of a distinct, genetically given 'language faculty': if a language really is a fixed code of form-meaning correspondences, it would be impossible for the child to acquire tacit knowledge of a language by the unaided light of the fragmentary and conflicting 'evidence' constituted by the *parole* to which he is 'exposed'. Hence the idea that the child is equipped with function-specific mental machinery to help him in his task is seen to be a requirement imposed by taking languages to be fixed codes in the first place. On the other hand, while proclaiming in effect that if languages are fixed codes there must be a language faculty which enables them to be learned, Chomsky has at the same time taken cognizance of the fact that there are no fixed-code languages to be found in the observable world, to the extent of drawing the latter-day distinction between E- and I-languages. Thus it is admitted that the fixed codes with which Chomsky is concerned are private mental phenomena, with no particular bearing on what are publicly acknowledged as 'languages'. But if a language is treated, not as the communal property of a group, but as the psychological possession of an individual, then since the linguistic experience of every individual is unique, we may expect the language (the I-language) that he possesses to be at least slightly different from that of every other individual. And if no two speakers have exactly the same system, then clearly, no ready-made answer to the question how communication is possible is to be had by referring to shared possession of the system. Hence a tendency to play down the role of an account of communication in shaping a linguistic theory:

Communication is *a* function of language, not *the* function.

And it therefore follows that a theory whose methodology is derived from the idea that communication is *the* function of language must be considered suspect.

(Newmeyer 1983: 100)

There is a large irony here. For the Chomskyan idiolectalism that Newmeyer is espousing must surely be seen as a theory whose methodology is derived from the idea that communication is the function of language. The idea that languages are determinately structured systems of some kind has never been validated by a non-arbitrary, exhaustive statement of the structure of any such system. It is an article of faith, motivated by prior adoption of a particular account of communication. To withdraw the proposition that it is the function of such systems to make communication possible is to saw off the branch you are sitting on. For it leaves the idea that there are such systems bereft of any justification at all.

III

The implications for the study of synchronic and diachronic linguistic variation of the circle of ideas under discussion can best be approached by considering the role assigned to the individual language-user by theorists concerned with these matters. 'The locus of language and the place of the individual within linguistic theory is a basic but unresolved issue' (Romaine 1981: 103; 1982: 245).[12] It is an issue which arises in the course of attempts to provide a satisfactory conceptualization of the connection between (i) languages; (ii) the fact of linguistic variation;[13] and (iii) the first-order linguistic behaviour of the individual and its basis in his 'linguistic knowledge'. Is it possible to provide a framework of ideas into which these three elements can be properly integrated?

Many theorists and schools of theorists have concentrated on one of these factors to the exclusion of the other two, or on some combination of two to the exclusion of the third.

For instance, a framework of ideas about language which concentrates on linguistic variation (specifically, diachronic variation) is the tradition of historical and comparative linguistics inaugurated in Germany in the early nineteenth century. Historical linguistics in this tradition neither makes any (or, at least, any crucial) reference to the individual language-user, nor has any very specific concept of a language. Its characteristic statements are essentially 'speaker-free'.[14] To say, for example, that French *lion*

85

derives from Latin *leonem* is not to make a statement about the activities of any actual language-users. In attempting to explain how such a change came about one might refer in general terms to the dropping of declensional endings, the nasalization of vowels before nasal consonants, and so on; and one might even suggest rough dates for these occurrences. But statements along such lines will fall a long way short of providing a picture of how these phenomena connect up with the linguistic behaviour of individual speakers. The reason for this is obvious enough: historical linguistics of this kind operates, and necessarily operates, at such a level of abstraction from actual speech-events that, although it is recognized that it is in some sense the activities of language-users that have brought the changes about, there is no practical possibility of relating the changes to particular speakers and/or to their activities on particular occasions. As one introductory text puts it: 'Historical linguistics seeks to investigate and describe the way in which languages change or maintain their structure during the course of time' (Bynon 1977: 1). In this conception it is *languages* which do things or fail to do them, not speakers; and this for the good reason that if macro-historical linguistics is to be pursued at all, there is no other way of pursuing it.[15]

But there was always an uneasiness about the personification of languages involved here: for at least some historical linguists the language-user was only ever left out *faute de mieux*. To this nothing bears more striking witness than the reception accorded to the Saussurean doctrine of the idiosynchronic language-state, whereby a language is envisaged as an autonomous, self-contained system of signs, the value and function of any sign being determined by its relations with all the others. This conception of 'a language', and the concomitant Saussurean insistence on the 'priority' of synchronic over diachronic study, has been widely accepted by diachronists. As Anderson has it (1973: 11): 'The [historical] linguist must utilise current linguistic theories in descriptive [i.e. synchronic] studies of language in order to analyse change in terms of an accepted framework of what language is.' Of interest here is, first, the assumption that it is synchronists rather than diachronists who have the right to decide what is or is not 'an accepted framework of what language is';[16] and secondly, that this should be so even when the proposed framework is one which excludes the possibility in principle of providing any account of linguistic change at all. For if linguistic units are only recognizable in the first place in terms of their intra-systemic connections, there can be no question of establishing the diachronic relatedness of different units in different synchronic *états de langue*.

Faced with what King (1969: 32) has called 'this forbidding crisis of theory', it is legitimate to wonder why historical linguists did not circumvent the crisis by simply ignoring the Saussurean doctrine that gives rise to it. For it is by no means clear that it is a doctrine demanding assessment in the dimension of truth and falsity. To see this one has only to consider what response Saussure could have made to an objector who simply denied that languages are idiosynchronic systems. Challenged along such lines, he could scarcely have appealed to some body of data or evidence that might decide the issue in his favour. What emerges here is that we are not dealing with a fact about the nature of languages that Saussure has discovered, but with a postulated theoretical entity (the idiosynchronic language-system) to which Saussure proposes to attach the name 'a language' (*langue*). Moreover, even if the Saussurean doctrine were mistaken for something which might be true or false, there seems no reason why historical linguists should not have rejected it as false, precisely because it allows no theoretical room for the diachronic relationships they are interested in establishing.

Why Saussure's synchronic linguistics was accepted by many diachronists is a matter for speculation. One feature that may be relevant is that it is a linguistics which, at least in intention, accommodates the individual language-user, if not the individual speech-event. What seems to have impressed many philologists is Saussure's statement that 'to determine to what extent something is a reality, it is necessary and also sufficient to ascertain to what extent it exists as far as speaker-hearers of the language are concerned'[17] (Saussure 1922: 128), and the accompanying observation that one thing that could not be expected to be real as far as speaker-hearers, *qua* speaker-hearers, are concerned, is the history of their language. It may be argued, therefore, that in their attitude to Saussure philologists demonstrated their belief that linguistics should be speaker-centred so far as possible, and that a linguistics which claimed to be speaker-centred had an automatic right to theoretical priority.[18]

But the speaker-centredness of Saussure's linguistics turns out to be superficial. The Saussurean *langue* is a static system of correlations of forms (*signifiants*) with meanings (*signifiés*). The system is held to be uniform for the whole speech-community whose language it is. But given that not all members of the same speech-community appear to correlate precisely the same set of forms with precisely the same set of meanings, the uniform (homogeneous) *langue* has to be envisaged as 'a sort of average' ('une sorte de moyenne'), as Saussure puts it (1922: 29),[19] both derived from, and yet also the basis for, the linguistic behaviour of the individual.

For Saussure languages-as-such do not vary. The linguistic behaviour of the individual, however, does. The language-as-such, therefore, is not to be found in, or in the behaviour of, the individual. No individual language-user, strictly speaking, either knows or speaks or understands the language of the speech-community to which he belongs.

This has been perceived as unsatisfactory in at least two respects. First, it follows from the adoption of such a concept of a language that variation must be either ignored or else relegated to some branch of study other than linguistics proper. In the case of synchronic variation this is overtly conceded by Saussure; in the case of diachronic variation it is nonetheless true for being denied by Saussure. Second, it leaves the relation between language-users and languages somewhat obscure (beyond such enlightenment as may be derived from the idea that a language is *in some sense* the property of the community to which its speakers belong). That is, like the nineteenth-century philologists', Saussure's is a 'one-factor' theory. He has a clear conceptualization of 'languages', but does not make room for either the individual language-user or for linguistic variation in time and place.

Post-Saussurean theorists have tended to respond in one of three ways. The first involves changing Saussure's concept of a language in order to accommodate variation. The second involves changing its location, or ontological status, in order to render more perspicuous the relation of his language to the individual language-user. The third involves combining these changes. In other words, faced with the perceived unsatisfactoriness of the notion of a homogeneous language system located in the collective mind of a community, theorists have decided either (a) that languages are heterogeneous; or (b) that they are located in the individual mind of the language-user; or (c) that they are both heterogeneous and located in the individual mind of the language-user.

The first of these moves is, not unnaturally, characteristic of theorists whose interest appears to focus primarily on variation itself. For example, Weinreich, Labov, and Herzog argue as follows:

> It seems to us quite pointless to construct a theory of change which accepts as its input unnecessarily idealised and counterfactual descriptions of language-states. Long before predictive theories of language change can be attempted, it will be necessary to learn to see language – whether from a diachronic or from a synchronic vantage – as an object possessing orderly heterogeneity.
>
> The facts of heterogeneity have not so far jibed well with the structural approach to language . . . . For the more linguists became impressed with the existence of structure of language, and the more they bolstered this observation with deductive arguments about the functional advantages of structure, the more mysterious became the transition of a language from state to state. After all, if a language has to be structured in order to function efficiently, how do people continue to talk while the language changes, that is, while it passes through periods of lessened systematicity? Alternatively, if overriding pressures do force a language to change, and if communication is less efficient in the interim (as would deductively follow from the theory), why have such inefficiencies not been observed in practice?
>
> This, it seems to us, is the fundamental question with which a theory of language must cope. The solution, we will argue, lies in the direction of breaking down the identification of structuredness with homogeneity. The key to a rational conception of language change – indeed, of language itself – is the possibility of describing orderly differentiation of the language serving a community.
>
> (Weinreich *et al.* 1968: 100–1)

So the obstacle posed by the Saussurean concept of the homogeneous structured system to accounting for change is to be removed by substituting as the object of study a heterogeneous structured system.

But there is a quite general conceptual problem with 'breaking down the identification of structuredness with homogeneity'. The structuredness of a Saussurean homogeneous language-system resides in the fact that such a system consists of a set of linguistic

89

units ('signs'), each of which correlates a form with a meaning, interrelated in such a way that the signs are mutually determining. This means that they cannot be *identified* except by reference to their relations with the other signs in the system. In this conception the homogeneity of the system is not an optional feature, but a prerequisite for determining its structure and, indeed, for recognizing it as structured at all. In contrast, a heterogeneous system is presumably one which embraces inconsistent or conflicting correlations of forms with meanings. But it is unclear on what basis the units of such a system are to be established, or what is supposed to bring them together as the components of a unified structure.

What is more, substituting a heterogeneous structured system for a homogeneous one does not alleviate the obscurity of the relation of such a system to the individual. In the end, variationists of Labov's stamp have nothing to say about the individual and his linguistic behaviour:

> The construction of complete grammars for 'idiolects', even one's own, is a fruitless and unrewarding task; we now know enough about language in its social context to realise that the grammar of the speech community is more regular and systematic than the behaviour of any one individual. Unless the individual speech pattern is studied within the overall system of the community, it will appear as a mosaic of unaccountable and sporadic variation.
>
> (Labov 1969: 759)

So variationism *à la* Labov turns out on inspection to be another one-factor theory. Attention is concentrated on variation itself, but at the expense of a coherent account of 'a language', and of any account at all of the role of the individual language-user.

More promising is the second response to Saussure, which might be referred to as Chomskyan idiolectalism. This involves relocating the language system in the individual mind of the language-user. Doing that provides a clear characterization of 'a language'[20] (as a system of form-meaning correspondences located in the individual's mind) and of the relation of the individual to such a language (the language-user unconsciously knows it, and this unconscious knowledge is the basis for his linguistic behaviour). Whatever the demerits of this conception of languages and language-users, Chomskyan idiolectalism, as a two-factor theory, is to that extent an improvement on one-factor theories such as

Saussure's and Labov's. But the third factor is missing: notoriously, Chomskyan idiolectalism, no less than Saussurean collectivism, rests on the postulation for theoretical purposes of linguistic uniformity, for 'no clear principles are known that determine the range and character of possible variation for a particular individual. Indeed there is little reason to believe that such principles exist' (Chomsky 1980: 218).

Hence the much-discussed difficulty a Chomskyan generative grammar has in handling certain kinds of synchronic variation which, it is argued, such a grammar cannot afford to ignore. An example is the variable deletion of word-final stops in English. Wolfram and Fasold (1974: 105) present data which show that word-final [d] is optionally deleted in an individual's speech to an extent which depends on (i) whether the stop is followed by a vowel; (ii) whether the syllable in which the stop occurs is stressed; and (iii) whether the stop is the past tense or past participle marker. Final [d] is most likely to be deleted in cases like *rapid stream* [ɹæpɪdstɹiːm], where the stop is followed by a consonant, occurs in an unstressed syllable, and is not a morphological formative. It is least likely to be deleted in cases like *tried it* [tɹɑɪdɪt], where none of these conditions obtains. The point is that the extent to which the [d] is deleted is systematically correlated with the three conditioning factors mentioned; and this state of affairs cannot be adequately dealt with merely by including in a grammar of English an optional rule of [d]-deletion. For such an optional rule takes no account of the fact that there are systematic degrees of optionality, determined by the linguistic environment of the [d]. The alternative is to incorporate into the grammar a so-called 'variable rule', which states the probability of occurrence of the different variants of the variable (in this case, presence or absence of the stop) as a function of different linguistic environments. If, further, it is claimed that variable rules are 'psychologically real' – that is, tacitly known by the individual as part of his linguistic competence – we have an extension of Chomskyan idiolectalism which incorporates the missing third factor.

A detailed discussion of these matters is to be found in Sterelny (1983). Sterelny objects to the incorporation of variable rules into generative grammars for a number of reasons. Chief among them is that interpreting variable rules as psychologically real for in-dividual speakers seems to imply that they count the number of occurrences of a given variant in their speech in order to make

NIGEL LOVE

their output tally with the statistical observations. The un-
likelihood of this forces Sterelny to consider the alternative
possibility that although the variable rule itself is not psychologically real, the observed systematic variability might be the
consequence of some other, hidden rule that is. Analogously the
fact that in serious chess white wins more often than black is not a
rule of chess, but is nonetheless the consequence of a rule of chess –
that white starts. But we can only say this because we can
demonstrate the connection between the rule and the consequence;
and in so far as, in the linguistic case, we cannot provide such a
demonstration, this alternative view offers no relief from the
implausibility of taking variable rules to be psychologically real.

Moreover, the claim that they are psychologically real appears to
depend on an unwarranted concentration on the role of the
speaker, as opposed to the hearer, in linguistic interaction. For the
rules of a generative grammar are supposed to be neutral with
respect to speakers and hearers. That is, they do not purport to
give an account of what is involved in speaking or hearing, but
merely provide a representation of the linguistic knowledge
brought to bear in acts of speaking and hearing. The idea that
variable rules might be psychologically real appears to violate this
neutrality, inasmuch as it is unclear what reality they could
possibly have for hearers. It is only if a generative grammar is
interpreted primarily as a model of the speaker's role in linguistic
interaction that the idea could ever be seriously entertained.

So much, it might be said, for this attempt at a three-factor
theory. But the paper in which Sterelny rejects it has a broader
interest in the present context. The structure of the relevant part of
his argument might be set out as follows. (1) Chomskyan-idiolectal
generative grammars represent facts about the structure of
languages. (2) It is a fact about the structure of English that word-
final stops are optionally deleted to an extent predictable from the
morphological nature of the stop and its phonological environment.
Therefore (3) a generative grammar should represent this fact.
Moreover (4) generative grammars purport to represent the
language-user's internalized competence. But (5) the formalization
proposed for representing such facts as the variable deletion of
word-final stops (that is, a probabilistic variable rule) is not
interpretable as a representation of the language-user's internalized
competence. Therefore (6) some alternative representation must be
devised.

What is most immediately interesting about this argument for present purposes is the conjunction of points (5) and (6). For what is Sterelny's objection to variable rules? Not that they do not represent the structural facts correctly, but that they cannot be psychologically real for individuals. But this objection must apply equally to the facts that variable rules embody; for a variable rule, like any other kind of generativist rule, is from one point of view no more than a way of stating the facts that it states. In other words, what is revealed by the psychological implausibility of variable rules is that it was a mistake to suppose that a psychologically real grammar ought to capture the facts that they state at all.

Sterelny's argument is interesting because it reveals an assumption basic to all the attempts canvassed here to elaborate an alternative to the historical philologists' focus on variation to the exclusion of languages and language-users. The assumption is that the central component of any such alternative must be an exhaustive account of the 'structural facts' of a synchronic language-state. The focus is switched to languages (conceived as synchronic language-states); language-users and linguistic variation must somehow be fitted in around them. In Saussure's case this is obvious enough: language-users only enter his conceptual world as imperfect repositories of the language they speak, while variation is no more than an accidental by-product of their attempts to speak it. In the case of variationists like Labov it is perhaps less obvious, for on the face of it variationists are primarily interested in variation itself. But variation is nonetheless seen as variation *within* an ordered structure. The emphasis on variation is not allowed to go so far that the very existence of ordered structures is called in question. On the contrary, the synchronic language state is still the real focus of attention: variation is allowed in by proclaiming that the synchronic language state is, in some theoretically obscure way, heterogeneous.[21] In the case of Chomskyan idiolectalists we see a reversion to the Saussurean insistence on homogeneity. A language is once more a self-consistent set of structural facts, located now in the mind of the language-user. But variation, both synchronic and diachronic, is once more banished by theoretical fiat. Those post-Chomskyan theorists who advocate the introduction into generative grammars of variable rules do so because they recognize that some structural facts about languages are, precisely, facts about variation. But the conflict between admitting such structural facts into the grammar and the requirement that the grammar be psychologically real is resolved in favour of the facts. In all these cases language-users and linguistic variation must accommodate themselves as best they can within an enterprise whose primary aim is a statement of the structural facts of synchronic language-systems.

Traditional historical linguistics is concerned with variation itself. Those theorists who have been interested in elaborating a linguistics which allows an adequate conceptualization of languages and of the role of individual language-users have been primarily concerned with languages. The third possibility – a primary concern with language-users – does not appear to have found much favour. Why should this be so? Why should dissatisfaction with the conceptual foundations of nineteenth-century philology take the form of a countervailing insistence on the 'priority' of the synchronic language system? An important strand in the answer is the closed circle of ideas with which we are concerned: the idea that communication is the swapping of messages in a fixed code.

Saussure's concept of the homogeneous language-system goes hand in glove with the code-using theory of communication. For him there must be a system, for it is the system which constitutes the code. The system must be homogeneous, for the code only explains how communication is possible if it is the same code for everyone. And it must be a social rather than an individual possession, because the individual's speech does not conform in all respects to the code.

Rejecting parts of this theoretical edifice while retaining others leads to problems. Variationists deny that the system is homogeneous. Idiolectalists deny that the system is found in the collective mind. Both these manoeuvres make it difficult to explain how use of the system permits communication. Idiolectalists, as we have seen, therefore further deny that permitting communication is the function of the system. But the system was only postulated in the first place because it explains communication.

From this conceptual mess one point emerges clearly enough. One reason that dissatisfaction with the conceptual foundations of traditional historical linguistics has taken the form of giving priority to the synchronic fixed code rather than to the individual language-user is that it has been taken for granted that preoccupation with the fixed code automatically caters for the role of the individual in relation to language. That role is to communicate with other members of the same speech-community by implementing knowledge of the fixed code. But there is no fixed code. And if there is no fixed code, then *a fortiori* communication is not a matter of swapping messages in it. What then is the speaker's role, and how does an adequate account of that role link up with a plausible account of linguistic variation?

Any attempt to answer this question must face the fact that no two utterances are identical in respect of either acoustic or communicational effect.

Any utterance of, for instance, *there's a dog howling in the yard* clearly differs acoustically from any utterance of *fish is good for you*. The differences between any such pair of utterances will be so gross as to be clearly represented in standard orthography and in any system of phonetic transcription. What is less immediately obvious is that any utterance of *there's a dog howling in the yard* will differ acoustically from any other utterance of *there's a dog howling in the yard*. This is less obvious because the differences will have no systematic representation either in spelling or in any except a very narrow phonetic transcription. Yet the evidence from experimental phonetics is clear: no two utterances are identical in respect of their 'phonic substance'.

As for non-identity of communicational effect, Taylor (1981: 11) offers an apposite illustration, with reference to the expression *what time is dinner?*:

> When Michael asks his mother 'what time is dinner?' she replies 'don't rush me dear, you mustn't be so impatient'. Yet when a guest, worried that traffic will make his arrival later than planned, asks Mrs Arbuthnot 'what time is dinner?', she responds 'Oh, some time around 7.30. We'll wait for you.' In the first case the question is taken as an instance of Michael's impatience at dinner time, whereas in the second case it is seen as a request for information. Still, we speak of the two utterances as being one and the same sentence, i.e. the same linguistic form, even though in each case the communicational content is different.

Given that every utterance is unique in respect of phonic substance ('form') and communicational effect ('meaning'), how can we avoid the conclusion that there are as many linguistic forms as there are utterances? Bloomfield, for one, responds by establishing at the outset what he calls 'the fundamental assumption of linguistics': namely, that 'in certain communities (speech communities) some speech-utterances are alike as to form and meaning' (Bloomfield 1935: 144).

For anyone who accepts this waving of the theoretician's magic wand as providing a solution in principle to the problem of how to identify the recurrent 'sames' necessary for the kind of linguistic analysis Bloomfield envisages, the obvious next question is how it is to be done in practice. *Which* speech-utterances are alike as to form and meaning?

The tenor of Bloomfield's discussion is such as to suggest that, for him, this was either never a serious question or, if it ever was, it has long since been satisfactorily answered – by the inventors of our writing system. Two utterances 'there's a dog howling in the yard' and 'there's a dog howling in the yard' count as 'alike as to form and meaning'. Two utterances 'what time is dinner?' and 'fish is good for you' count as unlike in both form and meaning. Whatever may be the criterion by which these judgements are arrived at, Bloomfield apparently sees no need for the linguistic theorist to examine them. Whoever invented alphabetic writing has already performed the necessary analysis: the linguist need do no more than take over its results as embodied in our standard spelling system. Part of the reason for this attitude is no doubt the fact that descriptive linguistics is itself an enterprise conducted largely in the written medium, which makes it difficult to get beyond the analysis that the medium itself imposes.[22]

Bloomfield does not, of course, explicitly admit that his would-be 'scientific' investigation of the structure of languages starts by assuming as unquestionably correct the analysis arrived at by those who first reduced languages to alphabetic writing. But it is nonetheless clear by implication, as when we are told that although morphemes are minimal meaningful combinations of phonemes, there are 'phonemes which do not appear in any morpheme, but only in grammatical arrangements of morphemes' (Bloomfield 1933: 162). The phonemes of which the morpheme *cat* consists will, in any actual utterance, be accompanied by one or more 'secondary' phonemes of stress, pitch, intonation, etc. As Bloomfield recognizes, there is no 'indifferent or abstract' form which consists of the morpheme *cat* without any accompanying secondary phonemes. Or, to put the point another way, there *is* such a form, but it is an abstraction, for which there is only one plausible source, the written word *cat*. The idea that stress, pitch, etc. are secondary, superficial flesh on a primary skeleton consisting of the morpheme *cat* in the abstract, seems to arise from the circumstance that orthography does not standardly provide any indication of stress, pitch, etc.

Bloomfield is not alone in assuming that the scriptic practices of a community provide a ready-made identification of the 'sames' required for an analysis of speech. It seems to be universally taken for granted, for purposes of describing languages, that the types instantiated by utterance-tokens are uncontroversially given by standard procedures of transcription. But the question that must be posed is whether this is true for language-users themselves.

It would be absurd to claim that language-use does not involve any distinction between types and tokens at all. To see why this is so, consider a necessary condition of generalizing discourse about anything whatever. In order to make general statements at all one must indulge in abstraction. Spatiotemporally distinct objects and events must be envisaged as 'the same' in some respect relevant to the purposes of the discourse. Something like a type-token analysis is required. If one is to talk about, say, cats, distinct individual organisms have to be seen as tokens of a type 'cat'. This is true for languages no less than for cats. For instance, for a question such as 'is *what time is dinner?* a grammatical English sentence?' to be even askable, one must avail oneself of the possibility of citing that form of words to indicate the object about which the question is being asked. This capacity of language to facilitate generalizing talk about the world is unremarkable, in the sense that it is so basic to our understanding of how language is used as to make it impossible to imagine what things would be like otherwise. It is a capacity made use of in our everyday talk about language itself. When A mishears B and asks him to repeat *exactly* what he said, B may understand A to be requesting, not the logical absurdity of an attempt to recapture the original unique utterance, nor even an acoustically identical replica of it, but merely another token of the same type. That is, that utterances can be treated as recurrent instantiations of underlying invariants is an assumption that we take for granted.

What is problematic is the further assumption that the analysis into types and tokens – what counts as an underlying invariant, and what counts as an instance of a particular invariant – is uniform for a whole linguistic community, determined for every member of that community by an abstraction called 'the language'.

Linguistic theorists sometimes demonstrate how problematic this assumption is, by ignoring it. Consider, for instance, Smith's (1973) study of his son's acquisition of English phonology. The general argument is that at all stages what is psychologically real for the child is the adult surface forms. The child's deviant pronunciations of adult words are explained by supposing that the adult forms are the input to a set of 'incompetence rules'; and the narrowing of the gap, as the child gets older, between his pronunciation and the adult's, is a matter of the progressive elimination of those rules. So, for instance, at 2 years 60 days the child had rules converting [tʰɛləfoun] to [dɛwibu], while at 2 years 260 days he was saying [tʰɛlibuːn], where the number of rules required to take him from [tʰɛləfoun] to his own pronunciation is rather smaller. Of interest here is what this account reveals about the linguist's assumptions. For Smith senior offers no explanation of how he is able, quite without hesitation, to take e.g. [dɛwibu] as a token of the type *telephone*. The question is not how he knows that [dɛwibu] *means* 'telephone', but what authorizes him to recognize it as instantiating the English word *telephone*. It is far from clear that any describer of English in general would admit [dɛwibu] as an acceptable realization of *telephone*, or that English-speakers, in other contexts, would be understood if they used it. Types and tokens are undeniably 'real' for speakers, but what the types and tokens are is something for speakers themselves to decide in particular contexts.

When A asks B to repeat *exactly* what he said, he is speaking metalinguistically. If, on the other hand, he merely asks him to repeat what he said, he is not necessarily speaking metalinguistically; and it is significant that now the response may be a different form of words entirely. All that is demanded in this case is another utterance perceived as similar to the first in respect of playing the same role in the communicational exchange. But that, in the end, is all that A gets even when he makes the more specific demand. He may *think* he is being offered a token of the same type (not that he would necessarily use that terminology). That is because he takes for granted the type-token distinction as a necessary concomitant of discourse about language. But if one asks what its being a token of the same type actually consists in, there is no answer, except that it conforms to the *idea* that it is: an idea validated ultimately by nothing more than the circumstances of the communicational interaction within which, and for purposes of which, it is entertained.

The view that language-use is a matter of deploying a pre-determined system of types and tokens is so entrenched that the two terms 'language' and 'a language' are often used interchangeably. Weinreich, Labov, and Herzog, for example, say that 'it will be necessary to learn to see *language* as an object possessing orderly heterogeneity', which only makes sense if for 'language' we substitute 'a language'. The same applies to the title of Katz (1981): *Language and Other Abstract Objects*. To take another example, the title of Cooper (1975), *Knowledge of Language*, suggests that the term 'language' is at least initially being apprehended in its 'mass' rather than its 'count' sense. But then, without further ado, the question of what knowledge of language might be is straightaway construed as the question: what is it to know *a* language? Similarly, in *Linguistic Behaviour*, Bennett (1976) starts off his preface by saying: 'this book presents in some detail a view of language – that is, language in general, not any particular tongue'. This at least recognizes that there is a distinction to be drawn. But then what immediately follows this preface is a discussion of an imaginary planet whose inhabitants have *a* language. But if we wish to understand the role of the individual in relation to language, it may be worth resisting this facile assimilation, at least until we have attempted to consider from first principles the relation between the two concepts 'language' and 'a language'.

The first point is that there is a sense in which 'language' has priority over 'languages'. This is true both as regards the origin of language in general, and as regards the linguistic initiation of the individual; and its truth depends on a simple point of logic. An initial act of understanding language must precede any analysis of the utterance concerned in terms of *a* language to which it might be held to belong. This is a point of logic in as much as the alternative view – that knowledge of the relevant language (or the relevant part of the relevant language) is a prerequisite for understanding an utterance – leads to an infinite regress. There is no way of getting started at all, unless a primordial A first says something and B understands it.

In this view the notion of *a* language (as distinct from language) arises with the perception – or idea – that utterances are repeatable. To embrace the possibility of 'saying the same thing' is automatically to introduce an abstraction underlying actual utterances: namely, the thing which is held to be repeated.

99

A collection of such abstractions may come to be codified and institutionalized.[23] Thus *a* language is created out of language. But the creation of a language in this sense is not the overt, conscious work either of individual language-users, or even of groups of language-users. This is not to deny that language-users themselves perceive repeatable abstract units underlying utterances, nor to deny that their 'decisions' as to how to analyse utterances in terms of such units are influenced by an institutionalized entity called 'the language'. The important issue is how these decisions relate to, and inform, their first-order language-use, as distinct from their second-order discourse about language-use. To analyse utterances in terms of the abstractions they manifest is to behave metalinguistically, not linguistically.

Perceiving utterances as manifestations of underlying 'sames' is not a necessary condition of any use of language whatever. It must be at least possible to understand an utterance without relating it to an antecedently given underlying abstraction. Nonetheless, once one has understood an utterance for the first time, one will entertain the possibility of repeating it. This involves *deciding* what would constitute repeating it.

At least one kind of linguistic variation arises from the fact that what counts as repeating an utterance is not fixed. An utterance does not somehow of itself indicate which of its features require imitation in order for a second utterance to be taken as 'the same'. What constitutes 'saying the same thing' depends on the kind of sameness required. At one end of the scale there may be situations in which saying 'je ne sais pas' counts as saying the same thing as 'I don't know'. Nearer the other end of the scale, the speaker of a certain variety of northern British English who asks a southerner to say [ɡɹæs] may consider that the southerner has failed to respond appropriately if he says [ɡɹɑːs]. Whether the utterance [ɡɹæs] is to be seen as instantiating an underlying abstraction which could alternatively be realized as [ɡɹɑːs], or whether the abstraction concerned is quite different from the one underlying [ɡɹɑːs], is not determinable in the abstract.

A language, as an individual's system of repeatable abstractions underlying language-use, is something that he creates for himself in the light of the constantly shifting situations in which he interprets and produces utterances. At no point, for him, does the system become fixed. (This is tantamount to saying that there is no system.) The abstractions underlying utterances, and hence what utterances count as 'the same', are matters for perpetually revisable decision.

The relation between languages, language-users, and linguistic variation is therefore this. A language is a second-order construct arising from an idea about first-order utterances: namely, that they are repeatable. Such a construct may be institutionalized and treated as *the* language of a community. But it remains a construct based on an idea: at no point does it become a first-order reality for individuals. (Although in a society which teaches its institutionalized construct to its members it may be expected to have a large effect on their first-order behaviour, and may perhaps give rise to linguistic theories which project the construct on to them as the basis for their first-order behaviour.)

Individuals, however, entertain the idea that utterances are repeatable. (After all, it is only because they do so that languages could ever be codified.) But the ways in which the idea can be implemented – that is, the abstractions that can be established by implementing it – are not fixed. Hence there arises variation. Variant abstractions may themselves come to be codified. Hence what is perceived as synchronic variation, and eventually, diachronic change.

The language-user's capacity to make different decisions as to what an utterance is an utterance of is both a source of variation and a bar to determining the individual's relation (*qua* first-order language-user) to an abstract system which can only be envisaged at all on the assumption that we already know what utterances are utterances of. Acknowledging this fact is one necessary step towards a satisfactory conceptualization of the relations between languages, language-users, and linguistic variation.

A second necessary step is to attempt to determine what has thus far stood in the way of acknowledging it. It would be facile to rest content, by way of response to this query, with pointing to the erroneous idea that languages are fixed codes designed to permit thought-transference. Why is that erroneous idea so pervasively influential?

IV

To say that every utterance is unique in respect of both acoustic and communicational effect is one way of asserting the indeterminacy of linguistic units. But that assertion is not entirely perspicuous as it stands. What are linguistic units, and what does it mean to assert their indeterminacy?

Linguistic units may be envisaged as the abstractions invoked in specifying what an utterance is an utterance *of*. In the most ordinary kind of case, the abstraction underlying an utterance is specified by producing another utterance which can be taken as identifying the type of which the first utterance was a token. Such a metalinguistic performance may or may not be underpinned by the use of explicitly metalinguistic expressions such as 'word', 'sentence', and so on. So, assuming for the sake of an example that A is producing a spoken discourse corresponding to this written text, if B asks A to repeat what he has just said, A might say, simply, 'and so on', or he might say 'I used the phrase *and so on*'. In either case A is specifying, or attempting to specify, the linguistic unit which underlay the original utterance. An organized practice of systematic talk about linguistic units clearly requires the extensive use of overtly metalinguistic expressions. (A linguistics which stopped short at specifying linguistic units merely by repeating utterances would not be very interesting.) Hence the analytic description of linguistic units in terms of such entities as phones, phonemes, morphs, words, sentences, etc. So we say that an utterance 'cats mew' is the utterance of a sequence of *phones* identified by writing certain symbols within square brackets which in turn manifest a sequence of English *phonemes*, identified by writing a marginally different series of symbols within slant brackets; it is the utterance of a sequence of English *morphs*, which in turn constitute English *words*, identified by writing certain symbols in italics, which in turn constitute an English *sentence*, whose grammatical structure can be shown, for instance by drawing the appropriate tree diagram with labelled nodes.

Now it might be said that the difference between identifying a type by repeating an utterance and identifying a type by talking about the words, sentences, etc. that the utterances realizes corresponds to the fact that if utterances are envisaged as tokens, they must be tokens of at least two distinct kinds of type. The distinction between a type and a token (that is, between a linguistic abstraction and its concrete realization) may be drawn with respect both to the relation between an utterance and the linguistic units it instantiates and an utterance and the utterance-type it instantiates. When you were invited to consider an utterance 'cats mew' just now, there was no utterance 'cats mew' to consider: all there was was an attempt to identify an utterance-type, and thereby to induce you to imagine that a token of that type had actually been produced. But that did not involve trying to specify a linguistic unit or combination of linguistic units. On the contrary, the aim was to cause the reader to imagine a naked utterance, unadorned by any analysis at all in terms of linguistic units. But although there is clearly room in principle for (at least) a three-way distinction between utterances, utterance-types, and linguistic units, for present purposes there is nothing to be gained by insisting on a distinction between two different kinds of abstraction, since in what follows attention will be focused on the relation between naked utterances and *any* kind of abstraction which utterances might be held to instantiate. That is, for present purposes the concept of an utterance-type may be subsumed under the concept of a linguistic unit: it will make no difference whether *cats mew* is thought of as the name of an English utterance-type, or as the name of an English sentence.[24]

What is involved in claiming that these abstractions are indeterminate? It should be said at the outset that there is nothing of interest to be gained from arguing about the indeterminacy of linguistic units in connection with analyses of particular utterances of theirs that particular utterers might choose to give on particular occasions. That is to say, it is presumably open to a speaker simply to provide (somehow) a determinate identification of the units underlying an utterance of his; and while we may wonder what he thinks he is doing in doing that, there would be little point in denying his right to live in a private world in which his utterances are the surface manifestation of a determinately structured idiolect, if he so chooses. The question of determinacy has to be raised against the background idea of a public language whose units, if they exist, are determined, or not determined, as the case may be, for all members of the community who share that language.

There are at least two rather different claims that might be made by someone who asserts, in respect of a communal language, the indeterminacy of linguistic units.

One would be the claim that although a language is indeed to be thought of as a system of abstract units, that system is not determinately identifiable because there are penumbral areas where doubt reigns either as to what the units are, or as to what the limits of the particular language are. A familiar example of the first kind of doubt is engendered by the difficulty of drawing a firm line between homonymy and polysemy. Is there in English a single noun *cat*, with (at least) both a restricted and a more extended sense? Or are there two different words which happen to have the same form? On the answer to that question, of course, will depend the size of the inventory of units of English identified at the word-level. Examples of the second kind of doubt are provided by generative grammarians when they stigmatize certain would-be sentences, not with the asterisk that indicates downright ill-formedness, but with the question mark that denotes doubt as to the grammatical status of the item in question.[25]

The second claim would be that utterances themselves are not determinately analysable by reference to a set of units, and that consequently, whether that set is determinately identifiable or not is either a question that simply does not arise, or one that only arises on a different plane of linguistic discourse from that which is concerned with the analysis of utterances themselves.

The difference between these two claims is that the first finds indeterminacy in the system of units itself, whereas the second finds indeterminacy attaching to the phenomena whose properties, it is alleged, lead to the setting up of a system of units in the first place. There is an obvious sense in which the second claim is more fundamental than the first; and it is this second claim that will be the focus of attention in what follows.

The claim is open to both a weak and a strong interpretation. At issue here is what is thought to follow from admitting it. For instance, for a variety of reasons it is often difficult to say which phoneme of a language a given stretch of utterance should be referred to. Is the schwa sound in the third syllable of an utterance 'I want to go' an instance of the phoneme that we have in the first and third syllables of *banana* or of the phoneme that we have at the end of *zoo*? As it stands the question is unanswerable, because the answer depends on how abstract a linguistic unit the phoneme is supposed to be; and that is a matter on which phonologists are divided. But the descriptive linguist can and does treat a problem of this kind as a mere local difficulty requiring from him simply a procedural decision as to how to apply his particular concep-tualization of the phoneme. As far as he is concerned, it need no more call into question the existence of the phoneme as a unit in terms of which languages are structured than the fact that there are places on the border between Belgium and the Netherlands whose location in one or the other has never been decided calls into question the existence of national boundaries as entities in terms of which the political world is structured.

That is, far from pointing to a need for a radical redefinition of his subject matter, indeterminacy is something that the linguist may well decide that he can live with. He is apparently not ineluctably bound to take it that the indeterminacy of linguistic units demonstrates their non-existence. On the contrary, he may feel free to hold that utterances are *for the most part* readily analysable as manifestations of abstract units, and that such units can be *more or less* reliably identified and inventoried at the various levels of linguistic description, and hence described in terms of the two planes of 'form' and 'meaning'. On this weak interpretation of the indeterminacy claim, the fact that linguistic units are in various ways hard to pin down, as illustrated earlier with respect to Bloomfield's theorizing about the morpheme, may simply be – and frequently is – admitted without any concomitant admission that indeterminacy destroys the theoretical basis for descriptive linguistics. That this indefensible attitude should be so widely adopted demonstrates the power of the fixed-code theory of languages in alliance with the thought-transference theory of communication.

In attempting to tease out the source of that power it is necessary to admit the cogency of the second, more radical indeterminacy claim (which means that the first, more trivial claim, falls away or at any rate becomes irrelevant), and of the strong interpretation of that claim. No viable descriptive science of spoken language can be based on the idea that utterances are to be understood as the outward manifestation of members of a determinate set of underlying abstractions. That is ultimately because utterances are not, as a matter of fact, the outward manifestation of members of a determinate set of underlying abstractions. Given the physical and circumstantial uniqueness of every utterance, the descriptive scientist has no basis for disengaging from the incessant flux of speech the recurrent invariants he is seeking. And given the human situation, there is no mechanism whereby language-use could have come to be a matter of producing and understanding tokens of such invariants. The idea of a language as a fixed set of abstractions raises the questions: who fixed them? How? When? It implies prior agreements. But there are no such prior agreements.

Language is radically indeterminate, as regards both what is meant and what is said. The use of spoken language involves an

NIGEL LOVE

incessant process of guesswork as to the significance of the vocal noises we hear one another make, against the background of such general ideas as we may entertain as to the sort of creatures we are and what, in given circumstances, our behaviour is likely to be. We communicate successfully by means of language to the extent that we achieve whatever may have been the purposes for which, on a particular occasion, we used it. But successful communication is not something for which there are criteria external to our own understanding of the interactional situation in which we find ourselves. A language is not a device which, if operated in accordance with the instruction manual, automatically yields something objectively discernible as 'communication'. To the extent that linguists describe structured systems of entities called 'languages' with a view to laying bare the nuts and bolts of the mechanisms with which we communicate, they are in error. There are no such things as languages, in this sense, to be described.

This is a reasonable starting-point for an account of the human situation *vis-à-vis* language. It provides a background against which to raise the question: 'Just what, in that case, *are* these entities called "languages" which have been thus summarily done away with?'

Suppose you have a tape recording of A's utterances so far. Now the radical indeterminacy claim implies the impossibility of analysing those utterances in terms of linguistic units: of saying what the utterances are utterances of, of saying what the phonemes, morphemes, etc. are. Yet it is manifestly the case that a competent phonetician could transcribe the recording, and that a competent phonologist could provide a phonemic analysis of the transcription; that any literate English speaker could, with a certain amount of editing, provide a corresponding stretch of written English prose, of which a syntactician could provide a grammatical analysis. In other words, there is a flourishing practice of analysis of utterances in terms of linguistic units, some phases of which can be undertaken by almost any literate lay speaker of the language in question, let alone by the professional academic linguist. How can this be possible, granted the truth of the radical indeterminacy claim? To answer that question would be to lay bare the dynamic of the fixed-code-cum-thought-transference theory of language and communication.

What must be squarely faced, in attempting to answer it, is that our practice of performing such metalinguistic operations as have

106

just been mentioned is as much a fact about the world of linguistic phenomena inhabited by members of societies such as ours as is the radical indeterminacy, with respect to descriptive linguistic analysis, of first-order utterances; and the two facts must somehow be brought into coherent conjunction if an adequate account of linguistic experience in such societies is to be had. What the linguist calls 'a language' cannot merely be dismissed as the result of his having made a lot of mistakes about the nature of his subject matter. Languages must, in other words, be naturalized.

One way of approaching this task is to consider certain logically imposed connections between utterances and abstractions.

However deep our ignorance about the origin of language, there are certain things one can reasonably say about it which do not depend on access to unavailable historical information. For instance, it can reasonably be said – as has already been said – that language must have started when a primordial A first spoke, and a primordial B understood. There is no question of B understanding A's utterance in virtue of being able to relate it to antecedently given abstract units, because there could not have been any. The first utterance logically cannot have been the utterance *of* something antecedently given.

So what can 'understanding', at this stage, mean? It means, perhaps, that A's vocal noise elicited from B behaviour that suggested to both A and B that associations (images, memories, etc.) somehow evoked in B by A's noise were similar to the associations of the noise for A.

Now all that happened, on the phenomenal level, is that a noise was made and certain behaviour ensued. And, in a sense, that is the beginning and the end of the story of spoken language: ever since, all that has ever happened is that noises have been made and behaviour has ensued.

But there is more to be said than that. The origin of language cannot have antedated the capacity in humans for reflecting on their experience. If using language is anything at all beyond making noises, language use presupposes that capacity. And there is no reason to doubt that A and B will have reflected rather furiously on this utterly novel experience. Thus the birth of language as an object of contemplation follows hard on the heels of the birth of language itself.

It is not a necessary feature of this account that A *intended* his noise to have the effect it had. In fact, it is hard to imagine how he could have, since there was *ex hypothesi* no established practice of eliciting certain behaviour from others by making vocal noises. But it is no less hard to imagine how even primitive man could have failed to entertain the notion – and sooner rather than later – that behaviour-eliciting vocal noises might be made on purpose. The obvious way to test this possibility would be to make a second, similar noise and see if it elicited a similar response.

Now there was no fixed criterion for deciding what might count as a 'similar' noise. (Nor has there subsequently ever been.) Nonetheless, if a range of similar noises was tried out and the predicted response, or type of response, was forthcoming, it is hard, again, to see how even primitive man could fail to entertain the idea of a *class* of noises, or type of noise, which would regularly elicit a class of responses, or type of response. Thus was the first linguistic unit invented. The defining characters of this unit were not fixed, and never would or could be. Nonetheless, the basic idea of an invariant abstraction – a class or a type – underlying utterances is a necessary feature of any attempt to make sense of even the most primitive linguistic event. If, as was suggested earlier, the essence of the concept of 'a language', as distinct from 'language', is the idea that there are things which utterances are utterances of, that idea is bound to arise as a result of no more than the human capacity for reflecting on experience, generalizing about it, and purposefully attempting to renew it.

This is one reason why the alternative to a linguistics based on languages as determinate sets of abstractions cannot be a linguistics of individual utterances themselves. That would leave out of account the fact that for language-users themselves, utterances are utterances *of* things. The problem is not the idea of abstractions underlying speech, but the idea of *determinate systems* of abstractions underlying speech. Where does this idea come from?

Language is characteristically used by communities with many more members than two. Language-users are not just participants in their own communicative acts, but also observers of the communicative acts of others. In respect of his own communicative acts, the individual will entertain shifting and tenuous notions of the abstractions instantiated by his own and his interlocutors' utterances. In the case of communicative acts of which he is a non-participating observer, if he understands them he may well relate the utterances involved to his own conception of comparable utterances in his own personal experience. But the important point is the development of a particular conception of what, in general, linguistic communication is for a whole community. Hence the emergence of a neutral observer's view of the linguistic process as a community-wide process. Such an observer's view is a crucial prerequisite for any idea of a language as a communal possession; and all that it requires is that individuals project on to others the kind of understanding they have developed of the linguistic interactions they themselves engage in. Note in particular that the existence of the observer's view is quite independent of the possibility of saying, for a large or infinite range of cases, *what* abstractions are in play in particular interactional episodes, and hence of articulating the supposed structure of a supposed communal language. So long as language is purely spoken language, there is no possibility of doing that, partly because purely spoken language is purely context-bound language, and partly because purely spoken language cannot yield the consistently reliable metalinguistic discourse required for articulating it.

The crucial difficulty where generalizing orally about linguistic experience is concerned is that we have nothing to do it in except utterances themselves. So how do we make clear that some of our utterances are to be taken as utterances, whereas others are to be taken as the names of something more abstract than utterances? One may suspect that primaeval attempts at talk about language were considerably hampered by the logically imposed fact that the names of utterance-types are, so to speak, homophonous with the corresponding utterances themselves. Nonetheless, some talk about language must have gone hand in hand with language itself from the very outset (as it does, of course, in the linguistic initiation of individuals today). Utterances are phenomenal events which play a role in interactional episodes. But they are also objects of contemplation. And if they can be contemplated, they can be talked about. But systematic talk about them requires a radically new development. That new development was the use of writing as a linguistic medium.

The first point to make about writing in this context is that the very fact it came to be used linguistically at all is evidence of a habit of trying to make sense of our linguistic behaviour by seeing it as involving the recurrent instantiation of abstractions. The notion that a non-phonic medium might be used to set down language already implies the idea of linguistic units as something more abstract than phonic utterances themselves. The inventors of phonetic alphabets have tried to circumvent the inherent abstraction-implying nature of writing by devising more and more detailed modifications of the alphabet in their quest for ever-narrower transcriptions. But there is no end to the search for the perfectly narrow transcription. Writing embodies from the outset the idea that languages are systems of abstractions: it cannot handle actual utterances at all.

Developing a written counterpart to spoken language removes the difficulties attaching to a purely oral practice of metalinguistic discourse. For although type-token ambiguities may arise for writing as for speech, writing provides a firm anchorage for at least one dimension of type-token distinctions, by providing a medium for displaying types which is different from the medium in which the corresponding tokens are produced. It introduces a new level of clarity into attempts to show what the abstractions are, by providing a system of types in terms of which, in literate societies, utterances will henceforth be interpreted.

Another important point about writing is that inscriptions are not bound to interactional contexts in the way that speech is. Their physical nature makes them both enduring and portable. How can these attributes be exploited in a practice of using writing to set down spoken language, given that the interpretation of spoken language is contextually determined? The answer is to combine the idea of utterances as the surface manifestation of underlying abstractions with the idea of a community-wide practice of utterance operating in this way, and simply *impose* a context-free oral interpretation on written forms.

Everyone already knew that his utterances, and presumably everyone else's, were utterances *of* something. The development of writing is not a matter of revealing what it was that utterances were utterances of, but of providing a basis for saying what, thereafter, utterances would be counted as utterances of.

How could it be otherwise? How could an appropriate set of units ever be abstracted from the utterances of a purely oral language? Given a certain indefinite range of different noises, and an indefinite range of variation as to their contextual interpretation, how could it be decided that one particular subset of elements from this variety should be gathered together, represented, referred to, or named as instances of a single entity embodied in a visually identifiable graphic form – let us say, CAT? It is hard to imagine even a potential answer to this question. But perhaps the question is unanswerable because it is wrongly put. Perhaps it was not a matter of the inventors of writing gathering together a variety of different individuals' privately entertained decontextualized linguistic abstractions and then supplying a written entity to label them. Perhaps it was the other way round: that is, a matter of providing a written entity which then defines, or – initially – points to, a range of actual and potential utterances with which it thereafter is to be associated.

If this is so, then there is a sense in which the linguistic use of writing involves the explicit reinvention or recreation of languages. It might have happened like this. Teaching a writing system involves oral explanation of the written forms. It involves (i) *saying* what piece of oral language certain graphic marks *are*, and conversely, (ii) indicating what graphic marks the system provides for writing a certain piece of oral language. But as far as the initial phases of the development of a linguistic writing system is concerned, only the first procedure is available. It makes no sense to ask 'How do I write *cat*?' until writing has been instituted. The instituting of it must be a matter of, as it might be, saying: 'if you do this (sc. write CAT), you write *cat*'. So what is meant by saying that writing involves the reinvention of language is that what linguistic interpretation is initially attached to a given inscription will depend on what the 'ur-writing demonstrator' can get his audience to understand by his oral explanation: that is, what range of images, associations, memories of similar utterances, etc. his meta-utterance conjures up for that particular audience on that particular occasion. This range is unlikely to be the same for each member of his audience, and is even less likely to match the range of images, etc. conjured up by similar utterances on other occasions to other audiences. So what CAT 'is' must at the outset be quite indeterminate. The first embryonic writing systems must have been semi-private modes of communication. But once a system has begun to be worked out, its use can and will come to be taught by means of the idea that particular utterances can be related to particular written forms. At this point writing achieves the object of fixing the interpretation of utterances (in the sense of providing them with something to stand as their name) by simply laying down what it is your utterance was an utterance of. If you write it CAT, then *that* is what you said.[26] And given the context-free, community-wide invariance of a writing system, the way is now open to the idea of a language as a context-free community-wide

111

system of signs, the indeterminacy of whose manifestation in speech itself can be explained as a mere imperfection of the oro-aural medium.

Writing thus eliminates the indeterminacy of spoken language, but only in the very general sense of eliminating, for a literate individual at least, doubts as to what abstractions he is supposed to refer what he says or hears to. In particular, it does not eliminate indeterminacy of interpretation. That, of course, never could be eliminated merely through the transposition of language into another medium of linguistic expression. So what fostered the idea, not only that the units of a language are determinately identifiable, but that associated with them there is a determinate interpretation, or sense, or meaning, such that it can seem reasonable to conceive of communication by means of language as a matter of causing that determinate interpretation, sense, or meaning to be evoked in the mind of one's interlocutor?

Answers to that question ramify in many directions. One non-negligible part of the answer is that determinacy of interpretation is an important buttress of the incalculably significant idea that by using language we can establish genuine knowledge of an outer reality that language *represents* to us. So determinacy of interpretation is ultimately part of an explanation of how it is that we are so successful at controlling and manipulating our environment. To descend to the linguistic particulars, one prerequisite for such a world-view is a practice of systematically describing languages. Setting out to do that depends, first, on the availability of writing, and second, on a transference of the context-independence of the written medium itself to what it is being used to describe. The practice of writing lies behind our capacity to think of a language as an object, detachable from communicational contexts, export-able, explicitly teachable to foreigners, etc. Implied here is the idea of a language as a self-contained system of communication, the meanings of the units of which are definable in terms of the system. A language is thus seen as a context-free medium or facility, invented by and in some respects under the control of its users, whereby we can, for instance, unambiguously articulate an understanding of the physical world. Writing made possible the expansion of our communicational universe by encouraging the idea that the vagaries of face-to-face communication in particular contexts were a mere circumstantial superimposition on the use of a system of communication whose determinacy was seen as guaranteed by the fact that linguistic types could at last be unambiguously defined, displayed, and discussed.

It is only with the advent of writing that the sort of systematic discourse about language that we call 'linguistics' becomes possible. Writing simultaneously invents languages as the objects of systematic linguistic description, and determines the shape of such descriptions. The descriptive medium itself articulates, grosso modo, the analysis which it sets forth.[27] It is this symbiosis of the medium and the object of study which makes the idea of languages as determinate systems of linguistic units seem so inescapable. Anyone who wishes to make the point that there is no such thing as a determinate unit of spoken English called *cat* runs up against the fact that in order to make it he seemingly has to invoke the unit whose existence he calls in question. As Pateman has put it (1987: 3): 'that we make use of iterable forms not defined by temporal co-ordinates seems presupposed by the very critique of that idea'.

Of the many good motives for redefining linguistics, one of the most pressing is the urge to extricate oneself from the conceptual straitjacket to which Pateman alludes. Given that getting out of it seems to be by no means straightforward, it might be useful to try to think about how we got into it in the first place. Thinking along the lines crudely sketched out in the foregoing paragraphs might indicate whether or how far there was ever any possibility of resisting it. There is a sense in which it must be a mere truism to say that every step along the way was a natural consequence of our attempts to understand and expand our linguistic experience. (Nobody forced us to adopt a particular way of thinking about linguistic phenomena.) But one point about truisms is that they are true; and this particular truth is one whose implications linguistic theory has persistently shied away from.

Any attempt to come to terms with language is bound to decontextualize it. In the history of language itself, a systematic decontextualization was first achieved via the invention of writing: that is, the systematic apprehending of oral utterances as abstractions amenable to representation in another medium. The reason the linguistics that naturally arises from this conceptual advance is inadequately equipped to understand contextualized language itself is that it automatically projects as first-order *realia* the products of the decontextualization process that made it possible in the first place. What is needed is a decontextualization which does not retroject itself on to the original context-bound situation as an *explanation* of the linguistic aspects of that situation. This seems to require a redefinition of the aspects of an interactional situation which ought to count as 'linguistic', thereby divorcing the descriptive metalanguage from the object of inquiry.

The two interlocking ideas which determine the conceptualization of 'languages' assumed in twentieth-century linguistic theory have a natural explanation in terms of the history of language-use itself. It follows that a conceivable redefinition of linguistics would be one whereby linguistics was in a sense seen as constituting its own subject matter. This would involve relocating the line between the linguistic and the metalinguistic. 'Languages' as structured systems of abstractions designed to allow thoughts to be conveyed from one mind to another should cease to be seen as the uncontentiously 'given' objects of linguistics. On the contrary, the processes whereby 'languages' in that sense come to have whatever existence they do have must themselves be the product of reflection on language: that is, of linguistics in a broader sense. In this conception linguistics started the moment human beings started to get to grips with their first-order linguistic experience, the ratiocinations of latter-day language experts being essentially continuous with that process. To have an understanding of that process would be to have the kind of higher-order perspective on our linguistic affairs whose achievement would be a worthwhile goal for a redefined linguistics.

NOTES

1   'faits de conscience, que nous appellerons *concepts*, se trouvent associés aux représentations des signes linguistiques ou images acoustiques servant à leur expression'.
2   See Baker and Hacker (1980: especially 595ff.) for general discussion of 'understanding', and Baker and Hacker (1984: 316ff.) for critical comment on the concept of understanding assumed by twentieth-century linguistic theory.
3   The term 'plereme' was introduced by Hockett (1958: 575) in the course of discussing 'duality' (i.e. double articulation) as a principle in terms of which communicational systems in general, and not just languages, are structured. Thus he says that 'morphemes are linguistic *pleremes*'. But 'plereme' may usefully be extended within linguistics itself as a cover-term for the various differing characterizations offered by theorists of the minimal unit of languages at the meaningful level of articulation.

4 For another example see the discussion of the Saussurean sign in Love (1984).

5 That is, of course, an isolated *-ing* being 'used', as opposed to 'mentioned'.

6 It is conceivable that habitual cranberry-growers sometimes call them 'crans'. This is not a possibility that Bloomfield envisages, but if necessary alternative examples of 'unique elements' could readily be cited.

7 Alternatively, one might characterize an I-language as 'what a native speaker's linguistic knowledge is knowledge of', or 'the total output of his internalized grammar'. It is hard to see that it makes any difference whether one speaks in these terms or in those used in the text.

8 'The language of such a speech community [e.g. the nineteenth-century Russian aristocracy] would not be "pure" in the relevant sense, because it would not represent a single set of choices among the options permitted by U[niversal] G[rammar] [= general theory of grammar] but rather would include contradictory choices for certain of these options' (Chomsky 1986: 17). Chomsky says that the sense of 'pure' here 'must be made precise', and promises to return to the issue later. But he does not do so.

9 Fetched, in fact, from Jones (1979).

10 Some might think that Chomsky and Halle (1968) casts doubt on this last statement.

11 See e.g. Gellner (1985: 101).

12 On these matters see also Pateman (1983). Pateman quotes this remark as an epigraph to his paper.

13 This term is used, here and throughout, to cover both diachronic change, however conceived, and synchronic variation *stricto sensu*.

14 cf. Lass (1980: 121ff.).

15 This is not to claim that no writer in the tradition referred to here ever has anything to say about the speaker. On the contrary, see e.g. Sturtevant (1917) for discussion of 'psychological factors' in sound change, and a sketch of some issues involved in accounting for semantic variation, which locates its origin in the differing experiences of individuals. But such attempts to provide a link between the language user and variation start by accepting as 'given' e.g. a sound change on the one hand, or a form which may be subject to variation in meaning on the other; and this 'givenness' is a product of the 'speaker-free' mode in which the phenomena are initially apprehended.

16 But on this point see Itkonen (1983). Itkonen 'partitions linguistics into "autonomous" (descriptive, synchronic) and "non-autonomous" (explanatory, diachronic) parts; the former, describing the "what" of languages, is according to him logically prior to the latter, concerned with the "how" of linguistic behaviour' (Pateman 1985: 481).

17 'pour savoir dans quelle mesure une chose est une réalité, il faudra et il suffira de rechercher dans quelle mesure elle existe pour la conscience des sujets'.

18 This speculation is not intended to imply that the *Cours de linguistique générale* plunged philologists into an abyss of negative self-regard. By insisting on a strict separation of (speaker-centred) synchronic linguistics from (speaker-free) diachronic linguistics, Saussure may have been seen as simultaneously relieving them of an obligation to consider the language-user's point of view, and putting their own concerns on a sound theoretical footing.

19 Saussure's point here is not entirely clear. As Pateman observes (1983: 110–11): 'the idea of "a sort of average" is not the same as the idea of a complete system of which each individual knows only parts as I know only some of the words in the *Oxford English Dictionary*'.

20 As we have seen, for 'language' in this sense some theorists would nowadays substitute the terms 'grammar' or 'I-language'.

21 cf. Bailey's theory of the 'polylect' (see e.g. Bailey 1973).

22 Similar indeterminacies of unit-identification could in principle arise for the writing system itself, but in practice they do not. One reason is that the alphabet is a small finite set of units, explicitly taught as such to apprentice writers. One aspect of what Harris refers to (1980: 6–18) as the 'scriptism' endemic in modern linguistic theory is this projection of the unit-determinacy of alphabetic writing on to what such writing is taken to represent.

23 Considerations relevant to an account of how this might happen will be put forward in the following section of this chapter.

24 Taking such a line involves cutting through a great many issues concerning the application of the type-token distinction to language and languages. The fact is that there are indefinitely many dimensions in which such a distinction might be established (utterance-types might be identified with reference to voice-quality, for instance); but in what follows no account will be taken of the implications of that fact.

25 Also sometimes encountered is the prefix '%', which means 'accepted as well-formed by only a certain percentage of . . . speakers' (Radford 1988: 9).

26 Nothing in this schematic account of the development of writing should be taken to imply the historical primacy of the alphabet.

27 This might be illustrated as follows. A recent introduction to sociolinguistics (Downes 1984: 13–15) sets out, by way of giving a preliminary example of phonetic variation, the following pronunciations of the English word *butter*: (i) [bʌtə], (ii) [bʌdəʳ], (iii) [bʌʔə], (iv) [bʌʔəʳ], (v) [bʌdə]. (They are identified as (i) British 'received pronunciation', (ii) Canadian, and e.g. New York upper-middle-class, (iii) London working-class, (iv) west-country British, (v) New York working-class.) A crucial fact about the abstraction underlying these five variants of *butter* is that in spoken English it has no name. If the speaker of British RP is asked to name the yellow substance on the plate before him, he will say '[bʌtə]'. If asked to say what word he has just used, he will say '[bʌtə]'. The corresponding forms for the working-class Londoner will be '[bʌʔə]' and '[bʌʔə]'. The only

way to identify a word (or any other linguistic unit) in speech is to produce a particular phonetic realization of it. There is no superordinate pronunciation which is the pronunciation of 'the word itself', as distinct from one of its phonetic variants. What ties the five forms together – indeed, what makes it possible to see them as different versions of a single entity – is the fact that *written* English contains the invariant *butter*. A stable and consistent analysis of utterance-tokens in terms of the types that they instantiate would be impossible without the assistance afforded by writing in the form of a phonetically neutral notation with which to identify types.

4

NORMATIVITY AND LINGUISTIC FORM

Talbot J. Taylor

> In other words, the language itself is a form, not a substance. The importance of this truth cannot be overemphasised. For all our mistakes of terminology, all our incorrect ways of designating things belonging to the language originate in our unwittingly supposing that we are dealing with a substance when we deal with linguistic phenomena.
>
> (Saussure 1922: 169)

A redefined linguistics will undoubtedly retain some components of the previous definition. There is no reason to abandon previous insights, although the formulation of those insights may itself require some redefinition. To my mind, the most important insight in modern linguistics is that captured by the concept of linguistic form, an insight first formulated authoritatively in Saussure's *Cours de linguistique générale*. To understand and explain language it must be studied not just as a material (phonic or graphic) substance, not just as behaviour, nor just as a product of human biology. The force of what we could call Saussure's 'semiotic principle' is that to understand and explain language it must be studied as a means of making sense. Language *matters* to language-users in a way that distinguishes it from mere material, behavioural, or biological substance. The fact that language makes sense, that it matters to its users, is an essential feature of its character as a human phenomenon. And it is only as something that makes sense that language can be seen to have *form*.

The semiotic principle and the concept of linguistic form were crucial to the Saussurean revolution in the study of language. Nevertheless, for reasons I will discuss later, Saussure did not pursue this insight to its logical conclusion. If language has form only as a means of making sense and if it can only be explained as a sense-making human phenomenon, then a redefined linguistics must begin by reopening the issue of how, with language, humans make sense: how language matters to us. The main contention of the discussion below will be that an analysis of language as a sense-making phenomenon must include as a central component the study of the normative character of language. If language has form, it is precisely because it is a normative activity, an activity that matters to its participants because they *make* it do so. The perspective from which linguistic form appears is not statistical, biological, abstract, chronological, logical, or psychological: it is a moral and political perspective.

It is ironic that, before the advent of the institutionalized practice we call 'modern linguistics', the notion of language as a normative activity was central to discourse on language (i.e. what I will call 'metalinguistic discourse'). But the complex ideological process of defining modern linguistics as the scientific study of language involved the explicit exclusion of issues of linguistic normativity. To determine how best to redefine linguistics we must first examine how it came to be given its current definition. This paper will begin with just such an examination. The second part of the paper will suggest two crucial components to an adequate redefinition of linguistics. The final part of the paper will consist of remarks on the implications of redefining linguistics so that, once again, the normativity of language holds a central position.

I

In the *Essay concerning Human Understanding* (1690), John Locke argues that the 'imperfections' of language make it an insufficient vehicle of communicational understanding. Due to what he saw as the freedom of individual speakers to use any words they choose to signify their private thoughts, Locke argued that there is no way of knowing if a given speaker and hearer take the same words to signify the same thought. The freedom of the individual linguistic agent's will is thus perceived as a threat to linguistic intersubjectivity: a threat therefore to human understanding. As Locke explains:

> Every man has so inviolable a liberty to make words stand for what ideas he pleases that no one hath the power to make others have the same ideas in their minds that he has, when

they use the same words that he does. . . . And let me add
that, unless a man's words excite the same ideas in the hearer
which he makes them stand for in speaking, he does not
speak intelligibly.

(Locke 1690: III, ii, 8)

To make sense of Locke's argument, it is important to
distinguish between his concepts of voluntariness and arbitrariness.
As he uses the word, 'arbitrary' means that there is no determining
feature, in either the word or the idea for which it stands, which
necessitates that the two be linked together. 'Voluntary', on the
other hand, means that the use at any time of a given word to
stand for a given idea is the result of a free act of the speaker's will.
Attributing 'voluntariness' to signification means that the relationship between word and the idea for which it stands, arbitrary or
not, is forged by the individual speaker's will, and not by some
other determining force. For Locke, then, signification is an act: an
act performed in mental privacy by an individual speaking agent.
Signification is not a pre-existent relation between two entities.
Thus the voluntariness, privacy, arbitrariness, and individuality of
the semiotic act are threats to its intersubjectivity. For, if the
signification of what I utter is determined – freely, and privately –
by me, then there is no guarantee that my hearer will take my
utterances to signify what I take them to signify. Indeed, it is hard
to see how they could.

In this context, it is revealing to compare Locke's ideas on
linguistic voluntariness, presented in Book III of the *Essay*, with his
ideas on political freedom and constraint, as presented in the *Second
Treatise on Government*. Locke begins the *Second Treatise* by identifying
what he sees as the natural political powers and rights of the
individual:

To understand political power aright, and derive it from its
original, we must consider what estate all men are naturally
in, and that is, a state of perfect freedom to order actions, and
dispose of their possessions and persons as they think fit,
within the bounds of the law of Nature, without asking leave
or depending upon the will of any other man.

(Locke 1689: II, 4)

In the *Second Treatise*, this discussion of the political state of

120

nature is followed by a demonstration of the social and political chaos that would result were every individual given the full exercise of these natural powers and rights (that is, as Locke says, were every individual allowed 'to be the judge in (their) own case'). The roots of political norms are then traced to the individual's sacrifice of a share of their own natural freedoms and powers to the political authority of laws, the aim of this sacrifice being the avoidance of the social anarchy that would arise were every individual allowed the full exercise of their natural freedoms:

> For the end of civil society being to avoid and remedy those inconveniences of the state of Nature which necessarily follow from every man's being judge in his own case, by setting up a known authority to which every one of that society may appeal upon any injury received, or controversy that may arise, and which every one of the society ought to obey.
>
> (Locke 1689: VII, 90)

Locke thus complements his analysis of the individual's basic freedoms by a discussion of the necessity of normative constraints on those freedoms.

To return now to Locke's linguistic ideas: a crucial passage in the *Essay* comes in the 32nd chapter of Book II. Here, Locke suggests that man misunderstands the relationship between ideas, words, and things: assuming that relationship to be determinate, exhibiting what he calls a 'double conformity'. Ordinary people take it for granted *both* that their ideas conform to the things they are ideas of *and* that the idea they signify by a given word conforms to the idea other men signify by the same word. That is, I would ordinarily assume my idea of 'the sun' to conform to (to be an accurate representation of) the sun itself; and I would also assume that the idea I signify by the expression 'the sun' is the same as the idea other speakers of English signify by the same expression. Furthermore, we take it for granted that this relationship on which our agreement depends exists independently of us and of our actions. Perhaps we take the perfection of that relationship to be an inheritance from Adam, to be God-given, or to be a product of Nature. What is most important, and most dangerous to the progress of understanding, is that our daily activities take for granted its determinacy and its independence. For, as we have seen, Locke's argument is that the relationship between words, ideas, and things is *not* in fact ideal; instead that relationship depends on our own voluntary actions and choices. Language in this respect is 'imperfect': i.e. it does not match up to our assumption of its perfection. The ordinary assumption of the ideal double conformity is at the core of our misunderstanding of our epistemological status, the misunderstanding from which Locke must free his readers if they are to grasp the foundations of human knowledge.

However, analogous to his strategy in the *Second Treatise*, Locke does not stop at his demonstration that language is imperfect and is therefore *not* the ideally intersubjective vehicle of ideas implied by the double conformity assumption. He also offers practical remedies to the imperfection of language, in the form of prescriptive, normative constraints on the freedom of the linguistic agent's voluntary action. With the application of these remedies, language might become a more effective tool for the conveyance of ideas. In other words, the rhetorical format of Book III is both descriptive, describing the true, 'imperfect' nature of language and communication, and prescriptive: offering prescriptive rules the following of which (Locke believes) can take us some way towards making language the effective vehicle of communication we mistakenly assume it already to be.

In Book III, Chapter 11, Locke recommends five rules that should be followed to avoid the 'inconveniences' of the imperfection of language. These may be paraphrased as follows:

(1) Use no word without knowing what idea you make it stand for.

(2) Make sure your ideas are clear, distinct, and determinate.

(3) Where possible, follow common usage, especially that of those writers whose discourse appears to have the clearest notions.

(4) Where possible, declare the meanings of your words (in particular, define them).

(5) Do not vary the meanings you give to words.

It is not altogether obvious (to say the least) whether obeying these norms would suffice to make language the reliable vehicle of communication that Locke wants it to be. Nevertheless, regardless of their usefulness, it is clear that Locke takes a 'normative' view of language. The normative prescriptions offered in the *Essay*, by commonly restricting the basic linguistic freedom of a community of individual agents, are designed to avoid the communicational anarchy that would result if all individuals exercised their linguistic freedom to express themselves as they choose. In both the *Essay* and the *Second Treatise*, the analysis of the individual's basic freedoms is matched by a discussion of the necessity of common consent to normative constraints on those freedoms. In this sense I refer to them both as 'normative discourses'.

We should also note here that the prescription of norms presupposes a prior ascription of freedom to the individual agent, linguistic or political. For if we are not free, then we cannot choose to obey the recommended prescriptions. Signification remains, in the Lockean perspective, a free act of the will; but it is a voluntary act which the individual agent *should* make conform to socially-imposed norms. Locke's normative discourse on language is undoubtedly an authoritarian discourse in this respect.

It is instructive to compare Locke's perspective on language as a normative phenomenon with that of the two most influential proponents of modern linguistic science: Saussure and Chomsky. Although the scientific models advocated by Saussure and Chomsky are superficially quite dissimilar, they can be seen to share some common principles: namely, the exclusion of issues of agency, voluntariness, and normativity from the domain of linguistic science, precisely those issues which we have seen to characterize Lockean linguistics.

To begin with Saussure, the discussion of language in the *Cours de linguistique générale* is, of course, very different from Locke's moral discourse. (I will use the name 'Saussure' to refer to the author of the *Cours*, even though many of the characteristics of the position put forth in that work are best attributed to its editors, Bally and Sechehaye.) Saussure proposes a radically different view of the place of the individual agent in language, a view which has largely determined this century's neglect of the topics of agency and normativity within the academic discipline of linguistic science:

> The language (*la langue*) itself is not a function of the speaker.
> It is the product passively registered by the individual. (. . .)
> Speech (*parole*), on the contrary, is an individual act of the will and the intelligence.
>
> (Saussure 1922: 30)

Saussure's originality is to locate the exercise of the individual will in the domain of *parole* and, at the same time, to identify the semiotic system *langue* as the object of linguistic inquiry. *Parole* may involve the individual's exercise of the will, but *langue* and its constituent signs are seen as a passive inheritance from previous generations. At the same time, this means that issues of agency and the normativity of language are shunted on to the side track of the study of *parole*, not the primary subject matter of the Saussurean science of linguistics. Thus, for example, whereas Locke had envisaged the signifying connection between ideas and words as forged by the will of the individual speaker, i.e. as a voluntary connection (and therefore a connection to which may be applied the coercive pressures of norm establishment and enforcement); Saussure, on the other hand, takes this connection to be determined independently of the speaker's will (a position I will call 'linguistic determinism', in opposition to Locke's emphasis on the voluntariness of language). For Saussure, neither the speaker nor the hearer has any say in choosing which *signifiant* is to stand for which *signifié*. Consequently, from Saussure's perspective there is no basis for Locke's sceptical conclusion that a given speaker and hearer might not connect the same *signifié* to the same *signifiant*. For, says Saussure, this connection is not of their own making. It exists independently of them and so is the same for both of them.

By this break with the voluntarism of the Lockean tradition, modern linguistics was able to present itself not as a normative discourse with the aim of constraining the voluntary character of language, but as an objective science, with the autonomous and determinate object *langue* its object of scientific inquiry. And as a science, linguistics could sever its links to prescriptive grammar and lexicography, links founded on the emphasis of Locke and others on the nature of linguistic agency and on the consequent need of normative constraints in order to attain the communicational goals of social discourse.

We see here an example of the connection discussed by Harris (1981) between the notion of communication as a form of telementation (or thought-transfer) and that of a language as a fixed code making this transfer possible:

> In brief, the model of linguistic communication offered is as follows. Individuals are able to exchange their thoughts by means of words because – and insofar as – they have come to

understand and to adhere to a fixed public plan for doing so. The plan is based on recurrent instantiation of invariant items belonging to a set known to all members of the community.

(Harris 1981: 10)

Both Locke and Saussure would have agreed with this model of linguistic communication. The difference is that while Locke felt that this model does not represent an actual state of affairs but one to which we should aspire, and for which we should constrain the exercise of our natural linguistic freedoms, Saussure believed this model to represent an existent state of affairs, the way things really are. Consequently, Locke's aim is normative: his metalinguistic discourse has the purpose of constraining the behaviour of individual linguistic agents so that they may more closely approximate the model of language and communication described above. Saussure, on the other hand, has a descriptive goal: namely, to describe the general characteristics of the linguistic systems we already use in achieving communication. Furthermore, Saussure reasons that one characteristic that such a code must have in order to be an effective vehicle of telementation is independence of the will of the individual and of the group. Hence, because it is independent of the will, it cannot be subject to normative constraint:

No individual is able, even if he wished, to modify in any way a choice already established in the language. Nor can the linguistic community exercise its authority to change even a single word. The community, as much as the individual, is bound to its language.

(Saussure 1922: 104)

By denying a linguistic dimension to voluntariness (and thus also to normativity), Saussure is able to provide the fledgling science of linguistics with an autonomous and determinate object of inquiry, at the same time offering an answer to Locke's scepticism about the nature of linguistic communication. The result is that the transference of professional discourse on language from a normative to a descriptive mode is given its conclusive theoretical justification.

It is interesting to speculate how Locke might have reacted to

Saussurean linguistics. He might have pointed out that the Saussurean speaker is not only powerless with regard to her language, she also undertakes no moral or practical responsibility for any of its characteristics. For Saussurean determinism, by adopting what amounts to a social version of the 'double conformity' myth, lifts the burden of linguistic responsibility from the shoulders of the individual language-user. In the end, no one – whether individual or collectivity – shoulders any moral responsibility for their language, for as Saussure repeatedly points out, 'the sign eludes control by the will, whether of the individual or of society: that is its essential nature' (Saussure 1922: 34). And we could go one step further to point out that this means that if certain features of a given language disadvantage some of its speakers, that's just too bad. Nothing can be done about it, and no one is to blame. If our language refers to women with a term that means 'wife to man', then no individual or group bears any responsibility for the injuries that may be inflicted by the use of that term. After all, that's just what 'woman' *is* in our language!

What this in turn reveals is that individual responsibility is the other side of the coin to normativity. Viewing language and signification as a voluntary act means that the individual can be held responsible for that act and can also be subject to the imposition of norms. Negating the voluntariness of language negates the applicability of concepts of linguistic normativity and linguistic responsibility.

A different but related form of what I am calling 'linguistic determinism' underlies the generativist linguistics inspired by Noam Chomsky. Generativism focuses not on linguistic systems as such, but rather on knowledge of such systems and on the acquisition of that knowledge. Linguistic knowledge is conceived to exist independently of the will and of agency, as a mental state of the individual speaker/hearer. The individual is assumed to have no hand in the making of linguistic knowledge. Rather, linguistic knowledge develops by natural means from a set of fundamental grammatical principles ('universal grammar') which has its source in our human biological inheritance. The parameters of human linguistic competence are then fixed with particular values by means of experiential triggering of predetermined options. Only certain values are possible, as determined by universal grammar:

> Universal grammar is taken to be a characterization of the child's pre-linguistic initial state. Experience . . . serves to fix the parameters of universal grammar, providing a core grammar. . . .
>
> (Chomsky 1981: 7)

> Once the values of the parameters are set, the whole system is operative . . . we may think of universal grammar as an intricately structured system, but one that is only partially "wired up". The system is associated with a finite set of switches, each of which has a finite number of positions (perhaps two). Experience is required to set the switches. When they are set, the system functions. . . . When a particular language is determined by fixing the values of the parameters, the structure of each linguistic expression is determined. . . .
>
> (Chomsky 1986: 146)

> The transition from the initial state to the steady state takes place in a determinate fashion, with no conscious attention or choice. The transition is essentially uniform for individuals in a given speech community despite diverse experience.
>
> (Chomsky 1986: 51)

> The language that we then know is a system of principles with parameters fixed, along with a periphery of marked exceptions.
>
> (Chomsky 1986: 150–1)

The position illustrated above I will refer to as 'natural determinism', to distinguish it from what might be called the 'social determinism' of Saussure. Whereas for Saussure the *langue* which an individual inherits is determined by his/her membership of a particular linguistic community, for Chomsky the linguistic knowledge which an individual acquires is the product of a natural determinism interacting with experiential stimuli. In fact, Chomsky's form of determinism is only a contemporary manifestation of a current of naturalist determinism running straight through the western linguistic tradition from Cratylus, the Bible, Thomas of Erfurt, and Condillac to the Language Acquisition Device (cf. Harris and Taylor, 1989). Of course, it is important to see that Chomsky's naturalist determinism is concerned with the principles of grammar rather than, as is the case with most of the naturalist tradition, with the principles of semiotics. That is, Chomsky is not concerned with the connection between a word and its meaning but rather with the combinatory connection between a word and other words. This reflects the greater concern in generative linguistics with syntagmatics over paradigmatics. Nevertheless, the connection with questions about the foundations of intersubjectivity in language remains the same. That is, while the naturalism of Enlightenment thinkers such as Condillac was in part designed to explain the foundations of semiotic intersubjectivity (in reply to Locke's sceptical doubts about those foundations), Chomsky's grammatical naturalism is designed to explain how, in spite of what he calls 'the poverty of experience', children all acquire what is, in its structural essentials, the same grammar:

> The basic problem is that our (linguistic) knowledge is richly articulated and shared with others from the same speech community, whereas the data available are much too impoverished to determine it by any general procedure of induction, generalization, analogy, association, or whatever.
>
> (Chomsky 1986: 55)

> The system of universal grammar is so designed that given appropriate evidence, only a single candidate language is made available, this language being a specific realization of the principles of the initial state with certain options settled in one way or another by the presented evidence.
>
> (Chomsky 1986: 83–4)

In this respect there is also an interesting parallel between Chomsky and Locke. For they both argue that experience alone is not sufficient to guarantee linguistic intersubjectivity (although in Locke's case it is semiotic intersubjectivity which is at issue while for Chomsky it is grammatical intersubjectivity). However, unlike Locke but like Saussure, Chomsky takes it for granted that linguistic intersubjectivity is a reality, i.e. that children from the same community do all acquire the same articulated linguistic knowledge, just as Saussure assumes that, for all the members of a given linguistic community, the same *signifiants* are linked to the same *signifiés*. For Locke this state of intersubjectivity does not currently exist and must be striven for in part by the normative constraint of the individual's natural linguistic abilities. Furthermore, connected to their common presupposition of linguistic intersubjectivity, both Saussurean structuralism and Chomskyan generativism take the object of linguistic science to be the investigation of that which makes linguistic intersubjectivity possible. For Saussure this is *langue*, conceived as a system of signs independent of the will of its speakers. For Chomsky it is the innate principles which ensure that, presented with similar experiences, the children of a given community will all acquire the same (or roughly similar) articulated forms of linguistic knowledge. Generative linguistics thus espouses a form of what I have called 'natural determinism' because it locates the source of linguistic intersubjectivity in facts of human biology; while Saussurean structuralism promotes a Durkheimian form of social determinacy, locating the source of linguistic intersubjectivity in the abstract social object *langue*.

Ironically, it speaks for the subliminal power of the communicational scepticism of Locke's *Essay* that, in spite of Chomsky's repeated attacks on empiricism, the link Locke establishes between experiential individualism and communicational intersubjectivity remains a primary motivating force in the development of contemporary generative theory.

In their common espousal of linguistic determinism, then, Saussurean and generativist theory share a common foundation. This foundation is at least partly inspired by the sceptical problem of linguistic intersubjectivity, a problem first developed in Locke's *Essay concerning Human Understanding*. Locke proposed a prescriptive solution to the problem of intersubjectivity with an argument based on a normativist view of language as an activity which is both voluntary and, because voluntary, subject to prescription and social coercion. Linguistic intersubjectivity thus becomes a moral and political responsibility. However, Saussure's structuralism defines the scientific object *langue* in such a way that it is immune to sceptical doubts about intersubjectivity: for the properties of *langue* are independent of the individual and the will. Chomsky's generativism, on the other hand, argues for biological determinism on the grounds that the shared properties of linguistic knowledge are too complex to be acquired by means of individual experience. In the one case, then, modern scientific linguistics protects language from scepticism by a vacuum of autonomy and arbitrariness, while in the other language is given the privileged, supernatural status of a human genetic endowment. It is these anti-sceptical manoeuvres which give the outline to what we now think of as the modern science of language.

As an institutional descendent of these manoeuvres we have today an academically enshrined linguistic science which takes as its data a decontextualized, ahistorical, and autonomous product, ignoring the voluntary, contextualized actions of individual agents in producing that data. An analogy may help clarify our position. We may imagine the position of the modern linguistic scientist as similar to that of a Martian visitor to Earth, long after the disappearance of human civilization. She finds in the middle of a wrecked building hundreds of pages of what she takes to be print-out from a computer. She begins to analyse the sequences of symbols that are printed therein, taking as her goal the reconstruction of a hypothetical computer program which *could* have produced those sequences. Perhaps she finds similar piles of print-out in other bombed-out buildings and so attempts several such reconstructions. On her assumption that each is the output of a different program, she may even attempt to determine the formal principles common to each of the hypothetical programs she reconstructs. Indeed, she might hope that she can uncover principles of such generality (e.g. the 'A-over-A principle') that they can be plausibly attributed to the hardware parameters of Earthling computers.

I hope that the sense of my analogy is clear. It is, I believe, easy to understand how such a project might hold a visiting Martian spellbound and how a Martian could hope that it would offer epistemic access to aspects of a culture otherwise hidden from Martian observation. After all, when all you have is a few piles of computer print-out on which to focus your desires, well, you might as well have a go.

But if my analogy *is* clear, then two points (at least) should emerge. First, the act of producing human language is nothing like the production of computer print-out. Computers have no choice when or what to produce. They do not have the option of breaking the rules of the programs under which they are operating. Nor are they subject to moral sanction. Their output is not held morally accountable by those who receive it. Computers do not have the choice of how to integrate their production within the (social and situational) circumstances in which they are made to produce. In sum, we take it to be one of the essential as well as one of the most useful characteristics of computer processes that they are completely determined. Yet it is only in the rarest of circumstances that we would ever speak of human linguistic production as completely determined. A way to focus on this point is to consider the familiar programmer's maxim: 'Computers don't make mistakes; people do'.

Second, we have as available data for linguistic research much more than a product analogous to computer print-out. Our analytical circumstances are not restricted in the way that our imaginary Martian's were. We can observe people producing language in interaction with other people within particular circumstances. We can watch them being taught how to speak, being corrected for making what are called 'mistakes', and being insulted, praised, classified, sanctioned, and even punished by others for the characteristics of their speech. We can investigate the complex network of beliefs that different groups entertain about the powers, purpose, and value of different features of linguistic acts. And we can inquire into the connections between those beliefs, their articulation and propagation, and the changing and varying characteristics of linguistic production itself. We can, that is, study the interaction of linguistic attitudes and linguistic behaviour in the political marketplace of everyday life. (That is, we can study language as a normative activity.) There is quite obviously nothing comparable in the study of computer print-out.

It is thus my general contention that modern linguistics, under the influence of what Harris (1981) calls 'the language myth', is based on question-begging foundations. Those foundations support what I have elsewhere called 'the principle of intersubjectivity' (see Taylor 1981: Ch. 6; Taylor and Cameron 1987: Ch. 8), a principle which leads Saussure to postulate the existence of an autonomous *langue* which it is the business of linguistic science to study and which leads Chomsky to postulate the existence of shared grammatical knowledge, the acquisition of which it is the business of linguistic science to explain. The way to address these foundational problems is to re-examine the notion of intersubjectivity, both semiotic and grammatical, and, by reconsidering the voluntariness of language, to address the question of linguistic normativity. It is this which I propose to do in the following section.

II

I want now to present a very different way of viewing the relationship between individual agency, understanding, and normativity (in part inspired by Wittgenstein's 'private language argument'). It is easiest to explain this different perspective by reference to an imaginary example. Late one night, listening to the radio in bed, Ronnie asks Nancy to close the window. That is, he says, 'Could you close the window, please?' Forthwith, Nancy gets up and closes the window. A few seconds after she gets back into bed Ronnie says in a stern voice, 'Did you understand what I said?' 'Yes dear,' she replies, 'I shut the window.' But little does poor Nancy know, this is just what Ronnie has been hoping she would say. For, while Nancy has been thoughtfully studying her horoscope, Ronnie has been watching a videotaped dramatization of Locke's *Essay* on the television. So, he quickly replies, 'But that doesn't prove anything! You can't *know* if you understood what I said. And I can't possibly know either. No one can. Really, dear, you've never understood a *word* I've said!'

In fact, Ronnie is being quite faithful to Locke in his challenge to Nancy. For, from the perspective of Locke's mentalist account of communication, even if we have observed this sequence of events, we still do not know whether Nancy understood what Ronnie said. Indeed, neither Ronnie nor Nancy can possibly know if Nancy correctly understood his request. To attain such knowledge one would have to perform the impossible: a comparison of the private ideas which Ronnie expressed by his words with those which Nancy privately took them to signify. Anything short of such a comparison of their private ideas would only amount to inductive evidence, which in itself cannot justify a claim to knowledge.

But there is something crucial left out in this reasoning. For requiring a mental criterion of understanding contravenes the normative practices of what we call 'speaking English'. Unless we put on our philosopher's cap, we usually have no problem in determining if someone understands what we say. And if a problem does arise we often have ordinary ways of resolving it. Communicational scepticism is simply not a regular feature of our linguistic experiences. Consequently, to impose, as Locke suggests, more stringent criteria on our use of the expressions *understand* and *know* than those we customarily place on that use is *not* to delve deeper into the hidden depths of the real meaning of those expressions or to discover what understanding and knowledge really are. Rather, it is to give new meanings to those expressions. So, Locke might be seen as creating the homonymic forms *understand$_2$* and *know$_2$*, different in use but identical in form to the ordinary *understand$_1$* and *know$_1$*. And this difference in use lies precisely in the requirement that the correctness of the application of the subscript$_2$ expressions can only be justified by comparison of speaker's and hearer's mental contents.

But we should see straightaway that analysis of the criteria for the correct use of these two new subscript$_2$ forms cannot be said to shed any light on the way the terms *understand* and *know* are ordinarily used by English speakers. If we give a new use to a word, we learn nothing about the *old* use by investigating the specific conditions for that *new* use. If I decided to use *black hole* to refer to chocolate milkshakes, it is easy to see that I would learn nothing about the ordinary use of that expression, about what it really means, or about the true nature of black holes (in the ordinary sense) by studying the physical characteristics of what I now refer to by the expression *black hole*. And yet Locke's scepticism about verbal understanding is based on using the expression *understanding* in a very different way than we ordinarily use it, i.e. giving it a new meaning. The sceptical doubts that Locke raises do not address features of that ordinary use.

So, the first lesson to be drawn from this imaginary drama is that Locke's communicational scepticism is unwarranted. Another way of putting this is that Locke's scepticism is not about understanding, but about a concept of mental convergence to which he has attached a new application of the word *understanding*.

But I want to be clear that this is not to say that it is impossible or intrinsically nonsensical to choose, as Locke does, to use the words *understand* and *know* in his own way. Anyone could, should they so desire, decide to use *understand* only to mean the identity of neurochemical events happening in the heads of both speaker and hearer. That is, making a word mean is a voluntary act, free from outside determination. Furthermore, they might go on to complain that no one can therefore ever tell if they or anyone else 'understands' (in this new sense of the word) what another says. But it would be nonsense to claim on the basis of this re-coining that, therefore, anyone who had ever said they knew they understood someone else had *in fact* been mistaken. For this would amount to saying that what other people had actually meant by *understand* (although involuntarily and without their being aware) was in fact the new meaning which we have just given to it. Such a claim would be as nonsensical as my complaining that the south bank of the Thames will not cash my cheques.

The point here, then, is that the purported non-identity of mental or neurological states is irrelevant to our ordinary, normative use of the expression *understand*. Consequently, it cannot serve to ground a sceptical appraisal of our use of that expression. And this in turn means that we do not require deterministic theories of *langue* or linguistic competence to defeat that scepticism. For what such theories attempt to explain is how verbal understanding *conceived as a form of mental convergence* could occur; and such a requirement is not imposed by our customary use of the expression *understand*.

This conclusion can also be applied to a sceptical question that might arise about the sharing of linguistic knowledge. Tom and Mary both, when presented with neologisms, add the same allomorphs of the past tense morpheme. After a present tense form ending in a voiceless consonant they both always add [t]. After one ending in a voiced consonant or a vowel, they both always add [d]. And after one ending in a [t] or a [d], they both always add [ɪd]. But the sceptic may ask, 'How can we be sure that they both share knowledge of the same morphophonemic rule? There are countless possible rules knowledge of which might lead one to produce the same results; we would need to compare the private contents of their individual minds in order to know if they do really both know the same rule.'

The reply to this scepticism about grammatical intersubjectivity is the same as that given to scepticism about semiotic intersubjectivity. The fact that Tom and Mary both produce the same past tense forms would ordinarily be taken as sufficient justification of the claim that they are both following, and therefore both know, the same rule. To impose more stringent criteria on the use of the expression *to know the same rule* is to have it mean something different than it ordinarily means: i.e. to have it mean something like 'be in the same mental or neurological state'. But discovering whether two people are in the same mental or neurological state is not ordinarily required in order to determine if they both know the same rule (or how could we ever know if two people both know the rules of tennis?). And to impose such a requirement on attributions of rule-knowledge would be to render nonsensical the countless everyday situations in which people have been said to know the same rules: e.g. 'Tom and Mary both know the rules for two-handed bridge because they both discarded all their face cards'. Knowing a rule (and thus knowing the same rule) is not a mysterious mental or neurological state, hidden behind the closed doors of mental privacy. If it were then our ordinary practice of attributing knowledge of rules (or of anything else for that matter) to agents would be nonsensical. And, if knowledge of a rule does not consist in a private mental or neurological state, then we need not speculate about how two or more individuals could come to acquire roughly the same private linguistic knowledge, nor develop hypotheses about the innate principles which they must share in order to make that acquisition possible.

Thus, when the concept of intersubjectivity is re-examined it becomes clear that there is no need to postulate abstract or social objects or to speculate about the acquisition of shared mental states in order to account for shared understanding of meanings or shared knowledge of rules. What we do need to examine are our ordinary practices of attributing and justifying attributions of shared knowledge, mutual understanding, and the like. These are the normative practices with which we forge the conformity, regularity, and multi-individuality of verbal interaction: i.e. by which we give the individual acts of verbal expression a social instrumentality. But in refocusing our attention on such normative practices, we turn away from speculation about abstract objects and mental states 'underlying' verbal interaction, and concentrate once again on language as a voluntary activity performed by individuals.

What does it mean to say that speaking (e.g.) English is a normative practice? Is what I propose here really just another form of determinism? Or Lockean prescriptivism?

To return to my imaginary drama, we might say that what is at issue here is the status of the grounds justifying Nancy's claim that she understood Ronnie's request to close the window. In addressing such issues, we should first observe what is customarily taken as sufficient justification of the claim that someone understands a given expression E. In fact, we ordinarily take someone's ability to explain the meaning of an expression, to respond appropriately to its use, or to use the expression in acceptable discourse as a criterion justifying the claim that they understand its meaning. In this respect I will refer to the 'criterial relations' between assertions such as 'he gave a correct explanation of E' and 'he understands E'. Part of knowing the meaning of the word *understand* is ordinarily taken to include knowing that the assertion of 'he gave a correct explanation of E' provides criterial support for the justifiable assertion of 'he understands E'. This criterial relation is similar to that between 'he always gets his sums right' and 'he understands how to add' or between 'he rides his bicycle to work every day' and 'he knows how to ride a bicycle'. In each of these examples, knowing what the latter statement means is customarily taken to include knowing that the former justifies its assertion.

But there is more to saying that a practice is normative for a community than that it is ordinarily performed. For that would only amount to a claim of the regularity of a practice and not of its normativity. So what is meant by saying that these ordinary criterial relations are normatively enforced?

The key here is that there is a moral weight given to the maintenance of such relations. They are taught to children and to other initiates into the community as the 'right' things to do. Their contravention is said to be 'wrong' and, on those grounds, may be subject to sanction. They are cited as justification for further actions and assertions. Normative criterial relations are, generally speaking, relations which the members of the community place a value on the maintenance of. They will to some extent try to maintain them in their own behaviour and to enforce them in the behaviour of others, although their concern and their value will very much depend on the situational context. Even teachers do not enforce grammatical norms all the time: for instance, while they are playing basketball with their friends. Furthermore, the members of the community will hold each other responsible for their maintenance. Anyone who says 'he always gets his sums right but I don't know if he understands how to add' breaks with an ordinary practice which speakers of English make a subject of moral enforcement. It is this that I mean by saying that, in so acting, such a person is contravening *a norm* of English speech.

In other words, we are in principle free as linguistic agents.

Meaning X by a given expression or combining that expression with others are both voluntary acts. But we do not live 'in principle'. We live in social contexts which function (to a large degree) by restricting the free exercise of our voluntary actions. If we regularly exercise our freedom to call anything by whatever word we like or to combine words however we choose, we may well find ourselves being 'corrected', sanctioned, or even ostracized. We are free, but we are also held morally responsible (and 'politically responsible', in the most general sense of the expression) for the public exercise of our freedom; and we in turn hold others responsible. Indeed, to some extent, for language to be socially useful, we need to do this: although the extent to which this is really required will vary greatly from context to context. This constant moral focus which is placed on our verbal behaviour is what brings us into the semblance of linguistic conformity that every speech community exhibits. That is, it makes us (mostly) all call *this* a 'tree' and *that* a 'bush' and say 'John ran' rather than 'John rans' or 'ran Johns'. To view such social conformity as having its source in underlying social objects or in natural determinism is to blind oneself to the everyday normative and political pressures by which we all (although some with much greater power than others) create and police that conformity ourselves.

So, in saying that such a criterial relation is a norm, what is meant is that that relation is subject to normative enforcement by the community. A norm in this sense does not exist in a Platonic third realm, forming part of our social inheritance, or as an abstract or theoretical object. Nor do they somehow have a natural, psychological, or biological source. Rather, to speak of norms is to refer to certain features of our day-to-day initiation into, participation in, and self-enforcement of, the moral characteristics of life in our community (or communities). So, to speak of the norms of language is thus to speak of holding people morally responsible for their linguistic performance. In so doing we draw attention to the role of language in the moral/political fabric that is everyday social interaction. We expect people to obey our norms; and if they do not, we look for a reason why. If no reason is forthcoming, we may well label those people 'confused', 'deviant', 'mistaken', or the like. Consistent non-conformity will probably lead not only to the application of such disapproving labels, but also to social ostracism. Part of being 'one of us' is submitting to the sort of coercive practices that make linguistic interaction a normative phenomenon. That is, the everyday political activity of enforcing our norms on our neighbours (and having those and others enforced on us) is one side of a social coin, the other side of which is the equally political activity of making them define themselves as one of 'us' or not as one of 'us'.

To view language as a normative practice is thus not to adopt a form of linguistic determinism (biological, psychological, or structural). Rather it emphasizes the location of the voluntary acts of individual linguistic agents within the coercive moral context of everyday life. The social conformity which we can observe in linguistic practice of individuals is thus not the product of a social or natural determinism; nor is it the shadow of an underlying shared object: biological, psychological, or social. Instead its source lies in the normative pressures individuals impose on those within and without their communities. That conformity comes from the social imposition of responsibility on the individual, not from the absence of moral responsibility embodied in determinism. To understand the regularity (as well as the irregularity) which characterizes verbal interaction we must therefore eschew the study of underlying determinate systems and instead study verbal interaction itself and the political and moral contexts from which verbal interaction cannot be separated. Such a study would immediately stand in opposition to the methods of generative and structural linguistics which, by de-contextualizing, formalizing, and 'idealizing' the patterned products of linguistic conformity, attempt to construct equally formal and ideal devices which could have generated, or are conceived as structurally immanent to, those patterns.

III

In the remainder of this paper, I want to expand on the points just raised by considering some of the implications of redefining linguistics in a way that recognizes the normative character of language. In the first place I think such a redefinition would allow us to make better sense of some themes in the history of linguistic ideas. For instance, structural and generative linguists pay scant attention to the earliest and perhaps most important linguistic treatise in the western tradition: that is, Plato's *Cratylus*. This is primarily because they cannot see the present-day relevance of its discussion of conventionalism and naturalism. And this in turn has its explanation in their neglect of the issues raised by a normative perspective on language, in particular the issues of correctness and authority. But if language is taken to be a normative, not an abstract or psychological, phenomenon then it is natural that the most salient issue for linguistic debate should have been the foundation of the notion of 'correctness' in language. The kinds of issues addressed in the *Cratylus* are the following. If it is not possible for us all to speak as we please (e.g. to use any names we choose to stand for things) and if we must therefore submit our speech to normative constraints, then *which* constraints should we follow? Do some constraints have a higher priority than others, and if so, why? What is the authority behind such constraints? Are arguments about the correctness of norms to be grounded in appeals to the authority of nature, logic, convention, religion, or tradition? Or is the only real authority that of political will? In this light the *Cratylus* can be seen as a component of Plato's attempt to rebut what he saw as the nihilism and political opportunism of the Sophists.

Not only does the contemporary neglect of such issues lead us to misunderstand the thought of earlier linguists who took them to be of prime importance. It also explains why the absence of such issues in contemporary linguistics should be perceived by 'the outside world' as a failure by academic linguistics to come to terms with the most important features of its own subject. For as the growing political prominence of linguistic issues today attests, notions such as that of 'correctness' are at the very heart of the lay public's concept of language. Consider the following excerpts from a newspaper editorial by a conservative educationalist, published in November 1988 by the London *Evening Standard*. Its author, John Rae, is commenting on suggested reforms in the way English is taught in school, as proposed in a report issued by the office of the Secretary of State of Education ('The Cox Report'):

> After 20 years of permissive education telling children there is no such thing as right and wrong, along comes a report on the teaching of English in primary schools that perpetuates this most damaging fallacy of the Sixties.
>
> At the heart of the report is a classic Sixties fallacy. It is argued that the accurate and grammatical use of English is no better than what the report calls "non-standard forms of

TALBOT J. TAYLOR

English". So that, if a child uses phrases such as "we was", "he ain't done it", "they never saw nobody". there is nothing "inherently wrong". Standard English turns those phrases into: "we were", "he has not done it", "they never saw anybody", but standard English, the report tells us, is just a dialect like any other. It should not be mistaken for correct English.

You could have fooled me. I thought it was correct to write "we were" and incorrect to write "we was". I did not realise it was just a question of dialect; I thought it was a question of grammar or, if you do not like that word, of logic. You cannot use the singular form of the verb with a plural pronoun.

The idea that children can be persuaded to learn standard English when they are told at the same time that it is no better than any other type of English is a typical intellectual conceit. Children want to know what is right and what is wrong.

Like most members of the lay public, Rae takes a normative view of language. He feels that there is a right and a wrong way of doing what we call 'speaking English' and 'writing English', and he wants teachers to teach their pupils what he believes to be the right way. Furthermore, he opposes his view to that of academic linguists who, as he sees it, deny that the normative concepts of 'right' and 'wrong' have any application to language. As he sees it (and as most introductory linguistic textbooks heartily agree), academic linguists simply give a scientific description of the rules of a given community's (or individual's) language, without attributing any normative values to those rules. This means, for instance, that the rules followed by those who speak what are called 'non-standard dialects' do not have, from the linguistic point of view, a different normative status or value than those used by the literate and educated speakers of the 'standard' dialect. And this is precisely because neither set of rules is seen to have any normative value at all, positive or negative.

Whatever one feels about Rae's politics, it is obvious that the linguist's argument about the value-free character of language will carry little weight with him or with those who make similar arguments, whether or not they share his political views. And it is not hard to see why. If our ordinary experience of language is as a normative activity, i.e. an activity in which such concepts as

140

'correct', 'right', 'wrong', 'good', and the like play an important role, then to assert that there is no right or wrong in language seems to run counter to our experience and, furthermore, to be irresponsible. Most teachers of linguistics know how difficult it is to persuade students to abandon their initial assumption that there is a right and a wrong to language. Perhaps this is because the students cling to what experience has taught them, at least until the authority of experience finally defers to the greater contextual authority of the professor's institutional status. (Ironically, what this shows is that at least the *meta*linguistic norms advocated by the professor do carry a much greater normative weight than those the student encounters in life outside class, in spite of what the professor says about the equality of norms.)

What Rae's editorial reveals is that modern linguistics has painted itself into a corner from which it can no longer carry on a meaningful dialogue with those who stubbornly resist the linguist's arguments that normative concepts do not have an application to language. Because modern linguistics does not place normative concepts at the centre of its inquiry, it simply cannot understand the values members of a culture will place on their linguistic practices – or why, for instance, people may become upset about the role they perceive language to be playing in their lives or in their communities. Such issues, from the perspective of modern linguistics, have nothing to do with the avowed concern of linguistic science to describe the contours of the object 'language' as a social or mental structure.

The general point here is that academic linguistics, by excluding the normative character of language from the cocoon of scientific autonomy, prevents itself from connecting up with or even understanding contemporary debates on the important political issues of language, i.e. on those aspects of language which really *matter* to speaker/hearers. Its inability to address the concerns of a conservative like Rae provides only one example of this impotence. For academic linguistics is no more able to address the concerns of feminists (cf. Cameron 1985) or the concerns of other progressive language-reformers (whatever their politics). Progressives and conservative reformers alike share a common recognition of the social, cultural, and political power of language, and of discourse *on* language, a power which has its source in the fact that language in the real world is, as Bourdieu (1982) argues, a highly valued economic (and political) property. And s/he who can determine the

141

relative values of different aspects of that property possesses a dominion of little equal in human affairs. No wonder language power is the source of daily and unrelenting struggle and is, if won even temporarily, jealously guarded.

In order to be able to engage with the important issues of the politics of language, regardless of the political positions espoused, academic linguistics must first come to grips with the fact that, *from the perspective of the language-user*, concepts such as 'right', 'wrong', 'good', and 'correct' (no less than 'word', 'meaning', and 'sentence') are necessary to an understanding of what language is.

In this case, a redefined linguistics must begin by reminding itself of Saussure's belief that the only appropriate perspective to take in the synchronic study of language is:

> that of the language-users; and its whole method consists of collecting evidence from them. In order to determine to what extent something is a reality, it is necessary and also sufficient to find out to what extent it exists as far as the language-users are concerned.
>
> (Saussure 1922: 128)

Only from the perspective of the language-user can we perceive what Saussure called 'linguistic form' (opposing it to 'linguistic substance'). It is linguistic form that makes language not a meaningless natural phenomenon, but rather a phenomenon with significance. This semiotic principle, the most fundamental in the structuralist revolution, has been forgotten in much of modern linguistic theorizing, due in no small way (and with great irony) to Saussure himself. For, it was Saussure's overriding aim to show how languages make communication possible, a feat which he attributed in part to the invariance and intersubjectivity of linguistic form. Consequently, Saussure assumed that linguistic form, that which is significant in language, must be the same for every member of a given speech community and must remain the same from speech situation to speech situation. In other words, Saussure assumed linguistic form to be psychologically and contextually invariant. Only by making such an assumption could the concept of a determinate linguistic form, and its opposition to that of infinitely variable substance, be the key to explaining how communication from one individual psychology to another could occur. Consequently, as I have argued above, Saussure removes linguistic form from the control of the human will and in so doing denies the relevance of normative concepts to an understanding of language and communication.

Generative linguistics has simply compounded this problem. For it finds grammatical intersubjectivity not in the concept of shared discriminatory perspectives on an infinitely variable verbal reality, but in common biological inheritance. In so doing, generativism abandons Saussure's semiotic principle that, to understand and explain language, linguistics must focus on how language *matters* to language-users, replacing it with a linguistics which treats language as a natural phenomenon, its semiotic potential thus being totally ignored as irrelevant to its analysis. From Saussure's point of view such a linguistics would be seen as a study not of linguistic form but of linguistic substance (and therefore would not be seen as worthy of the status of an autonomous discipline: for that which is distinctive about the linguistic treatment of language is, from Saussure's perspective, its focus on language as something that means).

Nevertheless, we must still see that if, according to Saussure's semiotic principle, the only perspective from which form, that which in language is significant, may be seen is that of the language-user, then a linguistics which does not place normative concepts at the heart of its conceptualization of language will miss that which makes language significant, thereby simultaneously missing that which gives language form. It is because language is normative that it *matters* to us, that it can be used to mean, that it has a communicational and a psychological instrumentality. Through normativity we make language significant; and, from the perspective of this significance, language has form. From any other perspective all that can be seen is what Saussure called substance.

In appreciating the force of Saussure's semiotic principle, a redefined linguistics must therefore begin with the realization that how language-users make language significant is irremediably contingent: depending on the individuality of person and of situation. What matters in my pronunciation in one situation will not matter in another, or to another person. Furthermore, whether and how features of my speech act matter can remain an 'open question', to be negotiated and perhaps fought over in the remainder of the interaction or in subsequent interactions. I may have 'meant nothing' by using *he* as the generic pronoun in my speech; but someone else may try to make it matter, either to me or to other people. In my defence I may cite the dictionary entry for *he*; others may oppose me by citing psychological studies of the kinds of assumptions people draw when 'generic' pronouns are used. The general point here is that what is significant in the speech event, and therefore what is form, is itself a matter of normative focus. How language 'matters' (in the largest sense) to its users is context- and person- and interaction-dependent; consequently, linguistic form is equally context-, person-, and interaction-dependent. It thus becomes apparent that, in a redefinition of linguistics, the semiotic perspective on language must undergo radical revision.

In this respect, Saussure might have done better by comparing language not to the economics of money but to that of property, e.g. land. What value the features of a given property have (its trees, its minerals, its soil, its location, etc.) is always to be determined. The value of my half acre is not determined in advance of a particular transaction. One buyer may feel I am too close to the road and so will only offer half the price of another who likes the ease of parking in front of the house. Or, on 'a good day' I may be able to talk up a potential buyer to a price far above what I could convince someone to pay on 'a bad day'. The general point here is that my half acre does not have a fixed value. (The state could fix its price but, note, not its value.) What value it has is contingent, dependent on the transactional context and on the likes, abilities, beliefs, prejudices, etc. of the participants in the transaction. Furthermore, what counts as a feature of that property, and a contribution to its value, is equally 'up for grabs'. Is the air above my half acre mine? Is the oil thousands of feet below it mine? Indeed the power to determine what counts as a feature of that property and the value of that feature will be greatly prized.

Academic linguistics currently operates on the naïve assumption that we all agree on our valuation of language, as well as on the features of language that carry value. Given this assumption the goal of linguistic analysis is simply to record those values and valued features. It is a lucky thing that the proclamations of linguists do not carry the same weight with political policy-makers as do those of economists.

Connected to the contingency of linguistic form is the contingency of what I have been calling norms. What norm applies in a given speech situation is open to contextual determination. The answer to the question 'What norm applies here?' does not somehow pre-exist the context in which the question occurs. And what answer is given is dependent on the relationship between the interactants, their beliefs and prejudices, their past experience, their 'pushiness', their political skills, and the like. Since the issue 'what norms apply here' is always 'up for grabs', it cannot therefore be the business of linguistics to describe the norms, e.g. of English, or of the lower middle class in New York, or of George Wolf, Esq. Such an enterprise would ignore their radical contingency.

Recognition of the normative character of language must also lead to an appreciation of the authoritarian status of academic linguistics (cf. Crowley 1989). Linguists are the 'experts' and from that institutional status gain a powerful position in the normative management of language itself. As such, scholarly discussion of language is a morally accountable part of language as a normative phenomenon. And it does no good for academic linguists, claiming scientific neutrality and autonomy, to attempt to deny that authority and consequent responsibility (cf. Chomsky 1979; Taylor 1990a). Such a claim is both morally evasive (at best) and intellectually naïve. Analogously, no one today is fooled into thinking, when political scientists present a purportedly 'unbiased' discussion of what they call 'the fundamental rights of man', that that analysis is *itself* politically neutral. And yet, under the influence of Saussure and Chomsky, we continue to mistake theories of the nature of languages and linguistic competence as culturally neutral and value-free, conceiving of ourselves as unbiased conveyors of scientific objectivity (cf. Newmeyer 1986; Taylor 1990b). But if we recognize the essential normativity of language (and its consequent inseparability from issues of power and ideology), then we will not ignore the fact that any institutional *discussion* of language is inseparable from the cultural context in which it occurs, a cultural context which *itself* is supported by and constrained by the normative practices of that culture's language. Academic linguistics is an attempt to make sense of language *within* our culture. It has an ineradicable link to our ordinary, normative linguistic practices; and (whether we like it or not) it is no more detachable from those practices than, as I have argued above, the concept of 'understanding' is detachable from the ordinary normative practices of attributing understanding to individuals and of evaluating, objecting to, and supporting such attributions (cf. Taylor 1986). Consequently, academic linguistics, as a decontextualized and institutionalized extension of our ordinary metalinguistic practices, cannot help but reflect, reproduce, and at the same time influence the prejudices, preconceptions, and ideologies of our culture.

Lastly, a redefined linguistics must once again recognize something that was clear to many who studied language before its nineteenth-century transformation into a descriptive/explanatory science: that the concepts of correctness, authority, and norm are crucial to the self-control by linguistic agents of their creative linguistic powers, of their expectations regarding the linguistic behaviour of others, and of their responses when their expectations are or are not met. In this case, a redefined linguistics will provide a new perspective on the question that looms largest in the modern study of language: i.e. why does language exhibit such a great degree of regularity? This question addresses what seem to be two quite different matters, both of which are absolutely central to orthodox linguistic concerns. On the one hand, there are questions such as: 'Why does everyone in this speech community pronounce "nurse" as [nɔɪs]?' and 'Why do they all agree that *soporific* means "tending to produce sleep"?' This sort of question addresses what we could call the 'external' regularity of language. These appear to differ from questions about what is seen as the 'internal' regularity of language: e.g. 'Why do nearly all words of this class ("adjectives") occur before words of this class ("nouns")?' Another version of the latter type of question would be: 'Why are all past tense morphemes voiced after vowels or voiced consonants and yet unvoiced after voiceless consonants?' Here the issue is not why everyone in a given community does something the same way but rather why they do so many different things the same way. Why, in other words, does language appear to be like a formal system?

It is perhaps easier to see how the former questions, concerning what I have loosely called 'external regularity', can be given new insight from a normative perspective on language (indeed this sort of perspective has a growing influence in contemporary sociolinguistics, cf. Cameron 1990). And yet it is for this very reason that the more formalist of linguists have argued that such questions are not 'interesting' and so have exiled them from the domain of linguistics 'proper', preferring linguistics to be an 'autonomous' science, focusing on the 'purely linguistic' questions of the internal regularity of language. The impulse behind such a restriction of focus is easily grasped. The internal regularities of language are most easily formalized if they are treated as *sui generis*, without 'external' motivation (hence the resistance to the 'importation' by variation theory and generative semantics of external concerns into linguistic explanation). And the formalization of such regularities seems more readily to allow for an application of the scientific methods of hypothesis-formation and verification. Furthermore, explanatory insight seems attainable by means of the formalization of rules and principles of greater and greater generality. And as the Martian analogy above suggests, the more such formalizations can be generalized, the more they appear to explain the regularities from which they were originally extrapolated. In other words, by restricting itself to the 'autonomous' perspective, focusing only on the internal regularities themselves, the most formalistic modes of contemporary linguistics believe that an explanation of those regularities can be achieved, i.e. a formal explanation (which then, depending on the deterministic tastes of the linguist, can be attributed to the abstract principles of language, to cognitive predisposition, or to biological inheritance.) The analogy to the Martian investigation of computer output is much closer to the truth than many linguists would care to admit.

But, resorting to such deterministic explanations of linguistic regularities, internal or external, based on a formalization of the products of verbal interactions, only masks the normative (and explanatory) source of those regularities in the everyday, humdrum political battles of will that make up the normative practices of verbal interaction. If the products of verbal interaction are amenable to formalization, this is because the context-dependent activities of producing are normative activities. The patterning of language is of our own making: to explain it we must examine it *in* the making.

We make each other conform our speech habits to the external regularities. And this in turn leads us to enforce 'internal' analogies on each other's linguistic production. If I know that I should pluralize /kæt/, /dɔg/, and /haʊs/ by adding the plural morpheme /s/, then when you pluralize /wug/ by saying /wugæ/ I may well 'correct' you, depending on the circumstances and on our relationship (etc.). And I may provide a justification for that 'correction' by referring to examples such as /kæts/ and /dɔgz/, or perhaps by reference to an explicit rule that I have been taught by authorities we both respect, e.g. teachers. Countless ways will be open to me to attempt to support my normative correction. Whether any will succeed remains to be seen. You may attempt to resist this norm-enforcing act; perhaps you will say that /wug/ comes from Latin where its plural form is /wugæ/. Or you may simply dismiss my authority in the matter. The rhetorical power of justification-by-analogy or of citing a general formalization of that analogy is a strong weapon in the normative enforcement of such 'internal' regularities.

In either case, 'internal' or 'external' regularity, we ourselves are the sources of our own verbal regularity. Thus, even the internal regularity of language has a social source: 'do like the rest of us or be wrong'. If we want to explain the formal regularity of what we produce in language, then we must recognize the normative character of the situated events of linguistic production. Regularity in language is merely the outcome of the place of linguistic events at the heart of the moral and political struggle between individual creativity and freedom and the social expectation and imposition of conformity. To treat the products of those acts as formally autonomous is to blind oneself to their significance: that is, to how they matter in human affairs. It is thus to fail to treat them as linguistic phenomena at all.

Agency, normativity, responsibility, authority, voluntariness, and correctness should therefore be central concepts in a redefined study of linguistic form. And yet, under the influence of its two founders, Saussure and Chomsky, modern linguistics has exiled such concepts from the explanatory domain of linguistic science. This is perhaps because they failed to realize that, if language is not conceived as a moral, political, and normative form of human activity, then it is not amenable to explanation at all.

5

THE EMERGENCE OF THE CATEGORY 'PROPER NAME' IN DISCOURSE

Paul Hopper

In *The Language Machine* (1987b) Roy Harris writes:

> The language myth of post-Renaissance European culture presents languages as fixed codes which enable individuals to communicate their thoughts to one another by means of words, and portrays linguistic communities as groups of individuals who use the same language. This is a myth which defines communication between human beings as thought-transference, and then postulates a social institution (the language) which makes that possible.
>
> (Harris 1987b: 7)

The 'fixed code', or 'determinacy', postulate about language is especially entrenched in modern linguistics. It results in a view of language as a set of a priori grammatical structures consisting of fixed categories, rules, and units, associated with fixed semantic correlates: fixed, that is, in advance of the speaker's use of them in discourse. Language is thus held to serve a 'telementational' end, enabling the exact reconstitution in the hearer's mind of a message originating in the speaker's mind.

If it can be shown that categories and units are not fixed, permanent entities in a finite system, but are always 'emergent' (Hopper, 1987, 1988), this picture of a language would be subject to serious revision. In Hopper and Thompson (1984) a view of the categories 'noun' and 'verb' was proposed in which the morphological, syntactic, and semantic criteria by which these categories are identified were shown to be secondary to their deployment in discourse. In such circumstances the concept of a category understood as a fixed, bounded entity was called into

149

question, and replaced by one of *categoriality*, the degree to which an entity conformed to a prototype (Noun, Verb) as defined by grammatical criteria. A hypothesis was formulated and argued for that the formal prototype would correspond to a prototypical discourse function for that category. Nouns, for example, were only fully identifiable as nouns when they were fulfilling a specific role, that of identifying new participants in a discourse; likewise, verbs were only decked out with the full set of morphological trappings identifying them as verbs when they functioned to report new events of the discourse. In other contexts, 'nouns' and 'verbs' were not accorded full categoriality, and (in ways that were manifested consistently though with different degrees of detail from language to language) showed a loss of morphosyntactic markings that suggested a lessening of categoriality.

The work referred to pointed to an essential lability in linguistic categories that left their membership open to what might be called 'negotiation', either (in interactive discourse) among participants in the discourse, or (in monologic discourse) among different types and strengths of reference.

In the present paper the question of the categorial status of Proper Names is discussed in the context of this openness, or indeterminacy, of categories.

PROPER NAMES IN LINGUISTICS, ANTHROPOLOGY, AND PHILOSOPHY

In a linguistic, logical, or semantic theory which includes a referential semantics there is something peculiarly central about proper names. One thinks of Frege, Russell, the early Wittgenstein and, more recently, Kripke, all of whom in one way or another take the proper name/individual relationship to be a prototype for the term/meaning relationship. Proper Names represent the quintessential example of a unitary form-meaning relationship, of 'terms whose meaning is exhausted by a one-to-one correspondence to particulars in reality' (Parret 1985). For any representational view of language, a name promises an ideal relationship of a fixed, stable, uniquely identified entity to an equally fixed and stable form; the semanticist's ideal of form and meaning as the two sides of the same coin. Consequently, the dislodging of this relationship is like the removal of a keystone from an arch. If the relationship of

150

individual to name is itself one of deferral, then the same must be true *a fortiori* of more obviously labile terms. Any emphasis on the social-interactive aspect of names to the downgrading of their supposed psychological-cognitive aspects is a move towards such a dislodgement; and similarly, the relativization of the grammatical category of Proper Name to discourse also involves a loosening of the privileged referential status of names. Although in this paper I shall be more concerned with the linguistic status of the category of Proper Name, I see this question as ultimately inseparable from other aspects of social and cultural naming behaviour.

The fixed, deterministic view of Proper Names has been dominant in most studies of naming. A considerable amount of work has therefore been devoted to the institutional sources of names in particular cultures. One of many examples is that of Evans (1977), who, in a study of naming among the Wagera, while describing a quite exotic naming practice, still presents a strategy for institutionalizing permanent names, and says nothing about what happens to those names after they are conferred or what other naming practices coexist with it. Still, some recent discussions, in particular of Personal Names, have emphasized social, cultural, and interactive rather than psychological cognitive aspects of the category. A number of others allow an indirect inference to be made about the actual use of names. I will mention briefly some of this work.

The study of personal reference by Sacks and Schegloff (1979) showed that in English conversational discourse, names function as 'recognitionals'; they are a handy single reference form and also function to pave the way for subsequent reference to a new personage. These two functions emerge from two principles described as *minimization* and *recipient design*, which are formulated as follows:

On occasions when reference is to be done, it should preferredly be done with a single reference form.   (16)

If they are possible, prefer recognitionals.   (17)

Here, 'recognitionals' are reference forms which 'invite and allow a recipient to find from some "referrer's-use-of-a-reference-form" on some "this-occasion-of-use" ' who is being referred to. Sacks and Schegloff note that names, especially first names, account for a very large number of such recognitionals. One of Sacks and Schegloff's examples illustrates the further point that an individual may 'have' (i.e. be referred to by) several names, which thus constitute a pool from which an appropriate recognitional may be negotiated:

A: Hello?
B: 'Lo.
B: Is Shorty there?
A: Ooo jest – Who?
B: Eddy?
B: Wood|ward?
A: |Oo jesta minnit. (1.5)
A: Its fer *you* dear.

(Sacks and Schegloff 1979: 20)

In his discussion of naming in Ilongot society (Philippines), Rosaldo (1980) points out that most treatments of names have understood them as 'classifiers' and 'slight their use in cultural performances'; Rosaldo shows that in fact '[n]aming people not only designates unique individuals and discriminates social categories, but it also shapes the quality of social interactions and reflects the dynamics of interpersonal histories.' One might even read a little more into Rosaldo's account (but no more, I believe, than is implicit there): it is precisely this social interactive, dynamic dimension of names which licenses their ability to uniquely identify and to discriminate social categories. It is not that there is an essential identifying-categorizing core to the name-person relationship upon which the interactional dimension is parasitic, but that such essence as may be ascribed to this relationship is precisely its provisional, negotiated status in social interaction.

Here too should be mentioned Geoffrey Benjamin's fascinating study of naming practices among the Temiar (Malayan Peninsula) (Benjamin 1968). Each individual has an 'autonym' (a unique, individual, personal name), formed, apparently randomly, from the residual morphophonemically possible word types which are not already exploited in the lexicon of the language. Individuals who are older or who are married come to be called by a birth-order name, which not only fits into a fairly complex taxonomic (genealogical) structure, but is itself loosely applied and, within limits, negotiable. Teknonymy (being named after one's children, i.e. 'father-of-X', 'mother-of-X') supplements this system, and there is also some necronymy (being named after a dead relative). In regard to the latter, Benjamin makes note of 'an apparent lack of fixity in the meanings of the names, recalling the looseness with which the birth-order names seem to be applied.' Individuals who have contact with the official world of written registers, licenses, etc. may moreover possess a Malay name. In Benjamin's careful account, and the same might be said of many other ethnographic accounts of names (but not of Rosaldo's), one especially misses a discussion of the discourse contexts which are conducive to the variations in naming to which he refers; yet one can infer without difficulty the existence of a social-interactive dimension to Temiar naming behaviour.

What Rosaldo notes from the perspective of anthropology, and Sacks and Schegloff from the perspective of sociology, Strawson (1974: 42) supports from philosophy in emphasizing the importance of the social aspects of naming, as opposed to its semantic individuating aspects, suggesting the following criteria for the use of a name:

(1) there is a circle or group of language users among whom there is frequent need or occasion to make identifying reference to a certain particular;

(2) there is interest in the continuing identity of the particular from occasion to occasion of reference;

(3) there is no short description or title of that particular which, because, say, of some fact about the relation of the particular to members of the circle, is always available and natural within the circle as a constant means of identifying reference to that particular.

Strawson's account, in so far as it introduces social criteria, represents an advance over the more conventional Fregean (etc.) analyses of names which understand them as functioning only in a referential-identifying mode. Nonetheless, ultimately the assumption of a fixed name-individual relationship dominates his treatment. Names are still referential labels which are permanent because of the need for fixed and stable reference across a variety of contexts. Strawson's analysis thus contrasts with that of the Sacks and Schegloff account, which stresses the particular discourse contexts in which recognitionals are favoured.

NAMES IN MONOLOGIC DISCOURSE

As I have pointed out, in Rosaldo's social-interactive treatment, names are not viewed as functioning primarily as referential-identifying forms, but as more labile and as more immediately symbolizing social relationships, often in an impromptu, improvised way: 'the semantic content of Ilongot names relates more profoundly to the interpersonal play of assertion and reply than to the structural properties of individuation and differentiation' (Rosaldo 1980: 22).

The importance of Rosaldo's insight about names as far as linguistics is concerned is this: names are like any other linguistic form, and are not privileged as quintessentially referential forms. Their place in the linguistic system is therefore just as much a matter of deferral as that of any other linguistic form – not yet fixed, and always subject to negotiation and withdrawal. If there is referential fixing of names, this is a fact about social institutions (possibly, for example, about bureaucracies supported by writing and printing), not a fact about human cognition and psychology.

In the remainder of this paper, I take up the idea of the lability, the inessentialness, of names from the point of view of monologic discourse.

In polylogic discourse names, then, exist as interactively emergent entities. It does not *necessarily* follow from this that they do not form a single, bounded category, one which is simply available to new members in appropriate social circumstances; yet if we bear in mind that according to Sacks and Schegloff names are part of a broader class of 'recognitionals', it would seem that this class must be allowed to include (for example) pronouns and adjectives, and perhaps intermediate categories also, i.e. to have only a loose and flexible correspondence with the standard categories of grammar. The same should be true of monologic discourse too: whatever category we are to assign names to should not be determined in advance, but should reflect the function of the 'recognitional' form in the text. And in fact this is what we do see, even in well-known English cases such as are discussed in any extended descriptive study. For example, Jespersen (1933: 164) states: 'it is impossible to draw a hard-and-fast line of demarcation between proper names and common names.' Nonetheless, Jespersen's examples of indeterminacy are of the fixed kind, involving geographical names like 'the Congo', and 'The

Strand'. As far as the categorial membership of proper names is concerned, Jespersen falls back on the standard view that 'proper names need no article, as they are definite enough in themselves' (1933: 164). Yet like other grammarians, Jespersen discusses examples in which names are accompanied by articles, adjectives, and other trappings characteristic of nouns.

Perhaps the chief drawback to the real insights offered by traditional grammar and by discussions such as that of Strawson is that they are based on hypothetical rather than actual textual examples. In recent years a number of strategies have been elaborated which might be used to counter this deficiency. For dialogic discourse observation and description of actual situations in which personal names have figured is needed; some of Rosaldo's work on naming in Ilongot society has provided a model for the study of naming behaviour. For the quantitative assessment of categoriality in monologic discourse, we now have the work of Givón on 'Topic Continuity', which has implications for the whole notion of 'referentiality' (Givón 1983). In this line of investigation, Givón and others use textual measures of such parameters as 'persistence' (the continued uninterrupted reference to a participant across a sequence of clauses) to make statements about the functions of various competing noun and verb forms in a language. Finally, the technique elaborated by Du Bois, in which the different distributional characteristics of pronouns and lexical nouns in discourse are computed, and their implications for grammar analysed, has been demonstrated in several important papers, most recently Du Bois (1987). A number of studies of different languages have been carried out using Du Bois' method (see Du Bois 1987 for literature). The present paper on proper names is an application of this work to the problem of categoriality in general and of names in particular.

Textual data are here examined to see whether personal names are a constant category or overlap categorially and functionally with other presumed linguistic categories such as nouns, pronouns, and demonstratives. The text used is a traditional Malay text, one of several which have recently become available through the Bibliotheca Indonesica series of the Royal Dutch Institute; it is the *Hikayat Sultan Ibrahim* (Jones 1983). The subject matter of the text is the saintly life of Sultan Ibrahim, who abandons a powerful throne to become an anonymous beggar, travels to Mecca, and eventually returns home to his wife and son.

155

If in dialogic discourse naming behaviour is held to have a social-interactive basis, in monologic discourse the use of names should be seen to compete with such other referentials as pronouns and ordinary nouns, and even alternative names, in order to sustain reference for the postulated reader or listener. In the text under consideration, the central character is referred to by several different linguistic forms:

sa-orang raja di-Negeri Irak bernama Sultan Ibrahim ibn Adham
'a certain king of the country of Iraq named Sultan Ibrahim ibn Adham'

This is the only time in the text that the Sultan is referred to by his full name. It is in the first sentence of the text, and he is first identified as 'a certain king [of the] country [of] Iraq', and then associated with his name, 'Sultan Ibrahim ibn Adham'. The verb *bernama* 'be called' is the usual way of making this association, which of course licenses the use of the name as a surrogate identifier or 'recognitional'. It is this surrogatory function which brings names as a category into competition with anaphoric pronouns and anaphoric nouns. The classifier *sa-orang* (translatable as 'a certain') typically accompanies human nouns which are relatively prominent and new to the discourse.

Sultan Ibrahim ibn Adham

The Title + Full Name is used after the initial mention only in direct discourse when Sultan Ibrahim is being referred to by other personages. It is thus evidently new to the presented discourse, i.e. functions as a prospective recognitional for the addressee of the direct discourse, but finds no use in the text addressed immediately to the reader.

Sultan Ibrahim

The simple Title + Name is frequently used. It is the 'narrator's voice' appellation, in other words, it is the prime recognitional for the text.

Sultan Ibrahim itu

This is the title supplemented with the deictic article *itu* 'the, that'. It is this deictic which identifies the title as a member of the category Noun so far as Malay is concerned.

baginda

Baginda (approximately, 'His Highness') is a title-pronoun of high respect, and is used in this text only in reference to Sultan Ibrahim.

baginda itu

The same title-pronoun accompanied by the deictic article *itu*. The uses of *itu* are discussed more fully below.

ia/dia/-nya

These are anaphoric pronouns. The first, *ia*, is intransitive subject; the second, *dia*, the transitive object; and *-nya*, written as an enclitic on the transitive verb, is the transitive agent (ergative).

To these must be added the *zero anaphor* (glossed '[0]'), which is occasionally found in highly continuous contexts, such as the following:

Maka segerah di-dapatkan-nya lalu 0 memberi salam [32]
'And straight away he fetched him and [0] made obeisance'

It can be seen that within this referential economy the proper name is not a clearly defined grammatico-semantic class. It shares with nouns the possibility of having a demonstrative; moreover, the name *Sultan Ibrahim* shares with the title/pronoun *baginda* the ability to uniquely identify one specific participant of the text, Sultan Ibrahim. Both *baginda* and *Sultan Ibrahim* may also be referred to anaphorically with the true pronouns *ia*, *-nya*, and *dia*. Like *Sultan Ibrahim*, *baginda* may have the deictic article *itu*.

In the text, too, names often function more like pronouns than their equivalents in other languages. The western reader is puzzled by the seemingly repetitious use of names in passages like:

Setelah di-dengar Shaikh Ismail bunyi orang minta buka pintu itu maka Shaikh Ismail pun segerah berbangkit lalu berjalan kepada pintu itu. Maka kata Shaikh Ismail 'Sultan Ibrahim kah itu?' [20]
'When Shaikh Ismail heard the voice of someone asking for the door to be opened, Shaikh Ismail at once got up and [0] went to the door. Then Shaikh Ismail said, "Is that Sultan Ibrahim?" '

157

PAUL HOPPER

Furthermore, names – but not nouns – may appear as agents of transitive verbs without the agentive preposition *oleh*, just like pronouns and the indefinite agent *orang* 'they, people'. The following examples illustrate the agentive construction with personal and anaphoric pronouns, and with the indefinite agent *orang*:

> dan lagi pula ibu-ku pun *ku*-tinggalkan seorang dirinya [34]
> 'Moreover, *I* have left my mother all alone.' [Pronoun *ku-*]

> Setelah sampai maka di-lihat-*nya* ada suatu sungai [16]
> 'When he got there, *he* saw that there was a river . . .'
> [Pronoun *-nya*]

> dan di-hampari *orang* lah daripada permadani dan suf sekelat
> . . . [44]
> 'and *they* spread out before him carpets and patterned woollen rugs . . .' [Indefinite pronoun agent *orang* 'they, people']

> Seketika lagi maka di-angkat *orang* lah hidangan berpuluh-puluh [44]
> 'Then straight away *they* served scores of different dishes of food.' [Same as previous example]

The following two examples show the use of a name without the agentive preposition *oleh*:

> Setelah di-dengar *Shaikh Ismail* bunyi orang minta buka pintu itu [20]
> 'When *Shaikh Ismail* heard the sound of someone opening the door, . . .'

> Maka lalu cincin itu di-persembahan *Muhammad Tahir* kepada raja [40]
> 'Then *Muhammad Tahir* handed the ring to the Regent.'

On the other hand, in the next example, the name is preceded by *oleh*:

> Setelah itu maka di-lihat oleh *Sultan Ibrahim* ada sepohon kayu di-tepi padang terlalu rendang [16]
> 'After that, *Sultan Ibrahim* noticed that there was a very small tree by the edge of the field.'

We see, then, names in the agent position aligning themselves grammatically sometimes with pronouns (lacking *oleh*) and sometimes with nouns (with *oleh*).

There is a more subtle, quantitative sense in which names behave more like pronouns than nouns. Consider first the following facts about pronouns, which, it will be recalled, may be objects (of verbs or of prepositions), transitive agents, or intransitive subjects. Numerically these are distributed in the text as follows:

OBJECT (*dia*)	7 (6.5%)
INTRANSITIVE SUBJECT (*ia*)	37 (34%)
TRANSITIVE AGENT (*-nya*)	64 (59.5%)

In other words, pronouns are preferentially transitive agents; a somewhat less favoured role for pronouns is that of intransitive subject; and pronouns are clearly strongly disfavoured as objects. The distribution of name and name plus demonstrative over the subject/object categories for two of the frequently occurring names is as follows:

	Number of occurrences	Number as topic/subject
Sultan Ibrahim	83	34 (40%)
Sultan Ibrahim itu	15	0
Muhammad Tahir	132	85 (64%)
Muhammad Tahir itu	17	0

A similar distribution prevails for the pronoun/title *baginda*:

	Number of occurrences	Number as topic/subject
baginda	78	50 (64%)
baginda itu	22	9 (41%)

Here again, the reference form with the deictic article *itu* is disfavoured for topic/subjects, although not as strikingly as with the names. The relatively low frequency of *Sultan Ibrahim* as topic/

PAUL HOPPER

subject (34/83, 40%) is attributable to the fact that many of the more anaphoric functions of the name have been assumed by the honorific pronoun *baginda* ('His Highness'). It will be recalled that *baginda* refers only to Sultan Ibrahim; its high frequency in the text accounts for the relatively low number of times the name *Sultan Ibrahim* occurs, but it has especially 'bled' instances where *Sultan Ibrahim* might have occurred as a topic/subject. Given a choice between *baginda* and *Sultan Ibrahim* in topic/subject function, the author leans towards the more pronoun-like form *baginda*. On the scale of pronoun-noun, then, *Sultan Ibrahim* occupies a position between *baginda* and *Sultan Ibrahim itu*:

dia/ia/-nya > baginda > Sultan Ibrahim > Sultan Ibrahim itu

Not unexpectedly, this scale conforms to Givón's 'scale of phonological size' (Givón 1983: 18–19) – the more topical elements are shorter than the less topical elements.

The disfavouring of the *itu* forms as topics is confirmed by the following distribution. The text contains numerous instances of the topic particle *pun*, which functions to explicitly topicalize an element which has dropped out of the discourse for a few clauses. *Baginda* occurs 31 times before *pun*, while *baginda itu* occurs only twice.

CONCLUSIONS

The statistics about the various 'recognitionals' in the text are revealing for the light they shed on the categorial status of these forms. Inferences which may be directly drawn are as follows:

(1)   The figures for the pronominal forms suggest strongly that the topic/subject slot favours pronouns.

Similar observations have been made by Du Bois in his study of texts in Sacapultec (Du Bois 1987). To these conclusions I would add a further inference, not immediately supported but surely reasonable: a preference for the topic/subject slot moves a reference form closer to the pronominal end of the pronoun-noun scale. In other words, the distribution can be treated as a criterion of association with the category pronoun or noun as the case may be.

(2)   The reference forms with the deictic article *itu* formally (i.e.

160

morphologically) resemble nouns, while the reference forms without the article formally resemble pronouns in that respect. The forms with *itu* moreover show a tendency to occur in positions other than topic/subject. (This distribution, incidentally, undermines any claim that a semantic feature such as 'human' or 'animate' is involved in topicality, except indirectly.)

Again, this conclusion is in harmony with Du Bois' observations. Nouns, i.e. lexical nouns, show a preference in texts for the 'absolutive' position, especially the transitive object.

(3)   Therefore, both the distribution of names (higher degree of preference for topic/subject) and their form (absence of deictic article) align them with pronouns. Their greater anaphoricity, as illustrated in the passage about Shaikh Ismail quoted, also pushes them closer to the pronoun class than is the case both in modern western languages and later Malay texts.

(4)   The 'names' accompanied by a deictic article, on the other hand, formally resemble nouns, and this formal resemblance is matched by the functional fact that they show a preference for object and oblique positions, the usual places for lexical nouns.

I have argued in this paper that Names are not to be disposed of either from the perspective of grammar as a discrete 'category' or from the perspective of meaning as fixed word/individual dyads. Instead they show a tendency to become assimilated to other word classes in direct response to the referential needs of the discourse, without being privileged referentially, and they are in a similar way functionally relativized to discourse context just like any other linguistic form. These two dimensions of the lability of names are not, I would suggest, independent of one another, but are both aspects of the provisionality of structure and its contextualization. The grammatical dimension is more obvious in monologic discourse like narrative, and the social interactive dimension in polyadic discourse; both are simultaneously present at a deeper level, functioning to establish and sustain referentiality in a negotiated social setting.

I would conclude by agreeing with Newton Garver that 'rhetoric and the context of actual communication are an essential and

PAUL HOPPER

ineradicable feature of all linguistic meaning' (1973: xxii). Proper Names, which ought, if anything is, to be categorially determined and to have fixed de-contextualized reference, seem in fact to be categorially quite labile and to be referential only, or at least chiefly, in a social and interactive context. This point of view is presumably at odds with one which insists, no matter how loose and negotiable the alleged structure turns out to be in everyday interactional practice, on invariant prescriptive models as structural sources of naming behaviour. By studying names not as predetermined, invariant nodes in a hypothesized socio-cultural or conceptual system, but as part of the speaker's repertoire of strategies for establishing and sustaining discourse contexts, the social meanings of names and their grammatical peculiarities can perhaps be brought into some kind of congruence.

REFERENCES

Anderson, J. M. (1973) *Structural Aspects of Language Change*, London: Longman.

Bailey, C. J. (1973) *Variation and Linguistic Theory*, Arlington: Center for Applied Linguistics.

Bailey, C. J. and Harris, Roy (1985) *Developmental Mechanisms of Language*, Oxford: Pergamon Press.

Baker, G. P. and Hacker, P. M. S. (1980) *Wittgenstein: Understanding and Meaning*, Oxford: Blackwell.

Baker, G. P. and Hacker, P. M. S. (1984) *Language, Sense and Nonsense: A critical investigation into modern theories of language*, Oxford: Blackwell.

Bartsch, R. and Vennemann, T. (1973) *Semantic Structures* (2nd edn), Frankfurt: Athenaum.

Benjamin, Geoffrey (1968) 'Temiar personal names', *Bijdragen tot de Taal-Land-, en Volkenkunde* 124 1:99–134.

Bennett, J. (1976) *Linguistic Behaviour*, Cambridge: Cambridge University Press.

Berwick, R. C. and Weinberg, A. S. (1984) *The Grammatical Basis of Linguistic Performance: Language Use and Acquisition*, Cambridge (Mass.): MIT Press.

Bloomfield, L. (1923) Review of *Cours de linguistique générale*, *Modern Language Journal*, 8: 317–19. (Reprinted in C. F. Hockett (ed.) (1987) *A Leonard Bloomfield Anthology*, Bloomington: Indiana University Press, p. 64.

Bloomfield, L. (1935) *Language*, London: Allen & Unwin.

Bolinger, Dwight and Sears, D. A. (1981) *Aspects of Language* (3rd edn), New York: Harcourt, Brace Jovanovich Inc.

Botha, R. P. (1987) *The Generative Garden Game: Challenging Chomsky at Conceptual Combat* (= *Stellenbosch Papers in Linguistics* 16), Stellenbosch: University of Stellenbosch.

Bourdieu, P. (1982) *Ce que parler veut dire*, Paris: Fayard.

Bynon, T. (1977) *Historical Linguistics*, Cambridge: Cambridge University Press.

Cairns, H. and Cairns, C. (1976) *Psycholinguistics*, New York: Holt, Rinehart & Winston.

REFERENCES

Cameron, D. (1985) *Feminism and Linguistic Theory*, London: Macmillan.

Cameron, D. (1990) 'Demythologising Sociolinguistics: Why language does not reflect society', in Joseph and Taylor (eds) (1990).

Carroll, John B. (1955) *The Study of Language*, Cambridge, Mass.: Harvard University Press.

Catford, J. C. (1969) 'J. R. Firth and British Linguistics', in Archibald Hill (ed.) *Linguistics Today*, New York: Basic Books, pp. 218–28.

Chafe, W. L. (1970) *Meaning and the Structure of Language*, Chicago: University of Chicago Press.

Chomsky, N. (1957) *Syntactic Structures*, The Hague: Mouton.

Chomsky, N. (1964) *Current Issues in Linguistic Theory*, The Hague: Mouton.

Chomsky, N. (1975) *The Logical Structure of Linguistic Theory*, New York: Plenum Press.

Chomsky, N. (1979) *Language and Responsibility*, New York: Pantheon.

Chomsky, N. (1980) *Rules and Representations*, New York: Columbia University Press.

Chomsky, N. (1981) *Lectures on Government and Binding*, Dordrecht: Foris.

Chomsky, N. (1983) 'On cognitive structures and their development: a reply to Piaget', in Piattelli-Palmarini (ed.) (1983), pp. 35–54.

Chomsky, N. (1986) *Knowledge of Language: Its Nature, Origin and Use*, New York: Praeger.

Chomsky, N. and Halle, M. (1968) *The Sound Pattern of English*, New York: Harper & Row.

Cooper, D. E. (1975) *Knowledge of Language*, Dorchester: Prism Press.

Crowley, T. (1989) *The Politics of Discourse*, London: Macmillan.

Crystal, David (1977) *What is Linguistics?*, London: Edward Arnold.

Crystal, David (1985) *A Dictionary of Linguistics and Phonetics* (2nd edn), Oxford: Basil Blackwell.

Culler, Jonathan (1987) 'Towards a linguistics of writing' in N. Fabb, D. Attridge, A. Durant and C. MacCabe (eds) *The Linguistics of Writing*, New York: Methuen, pp. 173–84.

Davis, Hayley G. (1989) 'What makes bad language bad?', *Language & Communication*, 9 1:1–9.

Denes, P. B. and Pinson, E. N. (1963) *The Speech Chain*, Garden City, NY: Doubleday.

Dewey, J. (1934, repr. 1980) *Art as Experience*, New York: George Allen & Unwin.

Downes, W. (1984) *Language and Society*, London: Fontana.

Du Bois, John W. (1987) 'The discourse basis of ergativity', *Language* 63 4:805–55.

Evans, Gareth (1977) 'The causal theory of names', in Stephen P. Schwartz (ed.) *Naming, Necessity, and Natural Kinds*, Ithaca: Cornell University Press, pp. 192–215.

Firth, J. R. (1935) 'The technique of semantics', in Firth (1957) pp. 7–33.

Firth, J. R. (1952) 'Linguistic analysis as a study of meaning', in F. R. Palmer (ed.) *Selected Papers of J. R. Firth 1952-9*, London: Longman, 1968, pp. 12–26.

Firth, J. R. (1957) *Papers in Linguistics 1934-51*, London: Oxford University Press.

Garver, Newton (1973) 'Preface' in Jacques Derrida *Speech and Phenomena, and other Essays on Husserl's Theory of Signs,* Evanston: Northwestern University Press.

Gellner, E. (1985) *The Psychoanalytic Movement,* London: Granada.

Givón, Talmy (ed.) (1983) *Topic Continuity in Discourse: A Quantitative Cross-language Study,* Amsterdam: Benjamins.

Harris, Roy (1980) *The Language Makers,* London: Duckworth.

Harris, Roy (1981) *The Language Myth,* London: Duckworth.

Harris, Roy (1983) 'Speech and language' in Roy Harris (ed.) *Approaches to Language,* Oxford: Pergamon Press, pp. 1–9.

Harris, Roy (1986) *The Origin of Writing,* London: Duckworth.

Harris, Roy (1987a) *Reading Saussure,* London: Duckworth.

Harris, Roy (1987b) *The Language Machine,* London: Duckworth (and Ithaca: Cornell University Press).

Harris, Roy and Taylor, T. J. (1989) *Landmarks in Linguistic Thought: The Western Tradition from Socrates to Saussure,* London: Routledge.

Harris, Z. S. (1951) *Methods in Structural Linguistics,* Chicago: University of Chicago Press.

Hockett, C. F. (1958) *A Course in Modern Linguistics,* New York: Macmillan.

Hopper, Paul (1987) 'Emergent grammar', in *Papers of the Annual Meeting of the Berkeley Linguistics Society,* 13:139–57.

Hopper, Paul (1988) 'Emergent grammar and the a-priori grammar postulate', in Deborah Tannen (ed.) *Linguistics in Context: Connecting, Observation, and Understanding,* Norwood, N.J.: Ablex Corp.

Hopper, Paul and Thompson, Sandra (1984) 'The discourse basis for lexical categories in Universal Grammar', *Language* 60 4:703–52.

Hudson, Richard (1984) *Invitation to Linguistics,* Oxford: Martin Robertson.

Hughes, John Paul (1967) *The Science of Language,* New York: Random House.

Itkonen, E. (1983) *Causality in Linguistic Theory,* Beckenham: Croom Helm.

Jespersen, Otto (1933) *Essentials of English Grammar,* New York: Holt.

Jones, M. (1979) 'The present condition of the Welsh language', in Stephens (ed.) (1979), pp. 112–30.

Jones, Russell (ed.) (1983) *Hikayat Sultan Ibrahim. The short version of the Malay text.* Dordrecht: Foris Publications. (Koninklijk Instituut voor Taal-, Land- en Volkenkunde: Bibliotheca Indonesica, 24).

Joseph, J. and Taylor, T. J. (eds) (1990) *Ideologies of Language,* London: Routledge.

Katz, J. J. (1966) *The Philosophy of Language,* New York: Harper & Row.

Katz, J. J. (1981) *Language and Other Abstract Objects,* Oxford: Blackwell.

King, R. D. (1969) *Historical Linguistics and Generative Grammar,* Englewood Cliffs: Prentice-Hall.

Labov, W. (1969) 'Contraction, deletion and inherent variability of the English copula', *Language* 45:715–62.

Labov, W. (1972) *Sociolinguistic Patterns,* Philadelphia: University of Pennsylvania Press.

Lass, R. (1980) *On Explaining Language Change,* Cambridge: Cambridge University Press.

Leech, G. (1974) *Semantics,* Harmondsworth: Penguin Books.

165

Lehmann, W. P. and Malkiel, Y. (eds) (1969) *Directions for Historical Linguistics*, Austin: University of Texas Press.

Lessing, G. E. (1766) *Laokoon* (translated by E. C. Beasley and H. Zimmern) in E. Bell (ed.) *Selected Prose Works of G. E. Lessing*, London: George Bell & Sons, 1879.

Lightfoot, D. (1982) *The Language Lottery: Toward a biology of grammars*, Cambridge (Mass.): MIT Press.

Lindemann, Erika (1982) *A Rhetoric for Writing Teachers*, New York: Oxford University Press.

Locke, J. (1689) *Two Treatises of Government*, ed. Peter Laslett, 2nd edn 1967, Cambridge: Cambridge University Press.

Locke, J. (1690) *Essay concerning Human Understanding*, ed. P. Nidditch 1975, Oxford: Oxford University Press.

Love, N. (1984) 'Psychologistic structuralism and the polylect', *Language & Communication* 4:225–40.

Love, N. (1988) 'The linguistic thought of J. R. Firth', in R. Harris (ed.) *Linguistic Thought in England 1914–1945*, London: Duckworth.

Love, N. (1990) 'Transcending Saussure', *Poetics Today*, 11.

Markus, R. (1982) 'Bridge', *Guardian Weekly* 5.12.82:23.

Newmeyer, F. (1983) *Grammatical Theory: Its Limits and Possibilities*, Chicago: University of Chicago Press.

Newmeyer, F. (1986) *The Politics of Linguistics*, Chicago: University of Chicago Press.

Parret, Herman (1985) 'Deixis and shifters after Jakobson', *First International Roman Jakobson Conference*, New York, 1985.

Pateman, T. (1983) 'What is a language?', *Language & Communication* 3:101–27.

Pateman, T. (1985) Review of Itkonen (1983), *Journal of Linguistics* 21: 481–7.

Pateman, T. (1987) *Language in Mind and Language in Society: Studies in Linguistic Reproduction*, Oxford: Clarendon Press.

Piattelli-Palmarini, M. (ed.) (1983) *Language and Learning: The Debate between Jean Piaget and Noam Chomsky*, London: Routledge.

Radford, A. (1988) *Transformational Grammar: A First Course*, Cambridge: Cambridge University Press.

Romaine, S. (1981) 'The status of variable rules in sociolinguistic theory', *Journal of Linguistics* 17:93–117.

Romaine, S. (1982) *Socio-historical Linguistics: Its Status and Methodology*, Cambridge: Cambridge University Press.

Rosaldo, Renato (1980) 'Ilongot naming: the play of associations', in E. Tooker and H. Conklin (eds) *Naming Systems*, St Paul, Minnesota: American Ethnological Society, pp. 11–24.

Sacks, Harvey and Schegloff, E. (1979) 'Two preferences in the organization of reference to persons in conversation and their interaction', in G. Psathas (ed.) *Everyday Language. Studies in Ethnomethodology*, New York: Irvington Publishers, pp. 15–22.

Sapir, Edward (1921) *Language*, New York: Harcourt, Brace & World.

Saussure, F. de (1922) *Cours de linguistique générale* (2nd edn), trans. Roy Harris, London: Duckworth, 1983.

REFERENCES

Searle, John R. (1969) *Speech Acts*, Cambridge: Cambridge University Press.

Smith, N.V. (1973) *The Acquisition of Phonology: A Case Study*, Cambridge: Cambridge University Press.

Stephens, M. (ed.) (1979) *The Welsh Language Today* (2nd edn), Llandysul: Gomer Press.

Sterelny, K. (1983) 'Linguistic theory and variable rules', *Language & Communication*, 3:47–69.

Strawson, P. F. (1974) *Subject and Predicate in Logic and Grammar*, London: Methuen.

Sturtevant, E. H. (1917) *Linguistic Change*, Chicago: University of Chicago Press.

Taylor, T. J. (1981) *Linguistic Theory and Structural Stylistics*, Oxford: Pergamon Press.

Taylor, T. J. (1986) 'Do you understand? Criteria of understanding in verbal interaction', *Language & Communication*, 6 3:171–80.

Taylor, T. J. (1990a) 'Which is to be master? The institutionalization of authority in the science of language', in Joseph and Taylor (eds) 1990.

Taylor, T. J. (1990b) Review of Newmeyer (1986), *Language* 66.

Taylor, T. J. and Cameron, D. (1987) *Analysing Conversation: Rules and Units in the Structure of Talk*, Oxford: Pergamon.

Weinreich, U., Labov, W. and Herzog, M. I. (1968) 'Empirical foundations for a theory of language change', in Lehmann and Malkiel (eds) (1969).

Wittgenstein, Ludwig (1953) (2nd edn 1958) *Philosophical Investigations*, trans. G. E. M. Anscombe, Oxford: Basil Blackwell.

Wolfram, W. and Fasold, R. (1974) *The Study of Social Dialect in American English*, Englewood Cliffs: Prentice-Hall.

INDEX

169

economics 51–2, 144
emergent 8, 149, 154
Evans 151
E[xternalized]-languages 69, 81–4
extralinguistic (factual)
  knowledge 3–4, 9, 55–7

feminism 10, 141
Firth 42–3, 58, 64
fixed code 6–8, 29–37, 41, 46, 57,
  84, 94–5, 101, 105–6, 124–5,
  149
Frege 150, 153

Garver 161–2
Gellner 155n.11
generative linguistics 25, 54,
  65–70, 75–82, 91–4, 126,
  128–30, 138, 143
Givon 155, 160
grammar 6, 12, 15, 17, 35, 45, 47,
  49, 51–2, 75, 82, 154–5, 161

Harris, R. 1–2, 6–7, 9, 17, 42,
  116n.22, 124–5, 131, 149
Harris and Taylor 9, 128
Harris, Z. 23–4, 76–7
historial linguistics 85–7, 94
Hockett 114n.3
homogeneous speech communities
  6, 30, 37, 88–9, 94
homonymy/polysemy 104
Hopper 8–9, 149
Hopper and Thompson 149–50
Hudson 10, 14–15
Hughes 13–14
Humboldt 9

ideal speaker-hearer 9, 37
idealization 4, 7, 36–8, 54–5, 69,
  72–3, 80–2, 138
idiolect 33, 36, 83, 85, 90–4, 103
ideology 9, 10, 12, 119, 145–6
idiosynchronic 86–7
imperfections of language 119,
  122
indeterminacy: of linguistic units
  100–7, 111–12, 116n.22; of
  Proper Names 150, 154–5

innovation 7, 34
integration 42, 44–52, 131
integrationalism 9, 44–52
interactive discourse 150–4, 156,
  161–2
I[nternalized]-languages 69–70,
  74, 81–4
intersubjectivity 119–20, 122,
  128–9, 131, 134–5, 142–3
invariance 46, 48, 97, 142
Itkonen 115n.16

Jespersen 154–5
Jones, M. 115n.9
Jones, R. 155

Katz 28, 99
Keynes 51–2
King 87
Kripke 150

Labov 5, 90, 91, 93
language: acquistion 4, 12, 54,
  65–70, 72–85, 127–8, 131, 135;
  faculty 11, 68–70, 73–5, 79,
  81–4; learning 12, 16, 33, 67–8,
  73, 78
langue 20, 33–5, 43, 53, 57, 87–8,
  123–4, 127, 129, 131, 134
Lass 115n.14
Leech 56
Lessing 39–40
Lightfoot 54–6
Lindemann 15–16
linearity 2, 7, 20–1, 25–6, 28,
  31–2, 39–41, 44–5, 48
linguistic: change 34, 86–7;
  competence 5, 91–2, 126–7,
  134, 145; form 47, 57–64, 95–6,
  118–19, 142–4, 148, 154, 161;
  knowledge 3, 6, 29, 33, 43,
  67–9, 72–3, 81, 85, 92, 126–9,
  134–5; sign 7, 9, 20–1, 24–5, 30,
  40, 44–5, 47–50, 52–3, 64, 86,
  90, 124; variation 5, 65, 85–101,
  115n.13
linguistique 19
literacy 6, 41–2
Locke 119–26, 128–9, 132–3

Stafford Library
Columbia College
10th and Rodgers
Columbia, MO 65216